Clyde Barrow *and* Bonnie Parker
Two Months Before They Were Killed

FUGITIVES

THE STORY OF

CLYDE BARROW
and
BONNIE PARKER

As Told by

BONNIE'S MOTHER *and* **CLYDE'S SISTER**
(Mrs. Emma Parker)   (Nell Barrow Cowan)

Compiled, Arranged, and Edited
by
JAN I. FORTUNE

Originally Published by The Ranger Press, Inc.
Dallas, Texas

First Printing, September, 1934

ISBN-10: 0977161056   ISBN-13: 978-0-9771610-5-8

Printed in the United States

All inquiries regarding this book should be addressed to
Wild Horse Press
4217 Arbor Gate Street • Fort Worth, TX 76133
Telephone - 254-797-2629
E-mail - wildhorsepress@att.net

www.WildHorsePress.com

Table of Contents

About the Book

Bonnie Parker and Clyde Barrow met their end May 23, 1934, but their exploits live on in dozens of books, movies and documentaries that are still produced to this day. *Fugitives: The Story of Clyde Barrow and Bonnie Parker* came rolling off of the presses in September of 1934, barely three months after the pair met their bloody demise.

The Barrow and Parker families fought hard against several media projects involving the telling of the Bonnie and Clyde saga. They filed a petition to stop the showing of a film produced shortly after the deaths of the criminal pair and also attempted to stop the sale of a record produced by the Southwestern Music Company and the R.C.A. Victor Company, Inc.

In their legal filings they made various claims including great mental suffering and embarrassment caused to the families and misrepresentation of Bonnie and Clyde. Yet, Bonnie's mother, Emma Parker and Clyde's sister, Nell Barrow Cowan, wasted no time in getting this book into print. Their stated desire was to tell the true story of their infamous kin, but no doubt there was a monetary goal as well.

The Ranger Press, Inc. in Dallas, Texas, was the original publisher and was a group effort with Parker and Cowan telling their stories to Jan I. Fortune, a noted poet, reporter and playwright in Dallas. In later years Fortune moved to Hollywood and worked on several movie scripts including *Dark Command*, starring John Wayne.

Both Clyde and especially Bonnie, were extremely close to their families. During the course of their crime spree, the pair roamed over much of the central United States, but always returned to Dallas and clandestine meetings with their families. The strain must have been tremendous on all involved since they were constantly watched by law enforcement authorities, who hoped to end the crime wave.

Several family members were arrested and tried for aiding and abetting Bonnie and Clyde. Both Bonnie's and Clyde's mothers served thirty day jail terms in 1935, almost a year after the death of the pair.

Mrs. Parker was especially protective of her son's legacy and even went as far as tearing down photos on display at a movie theater in Dallas. The Capital Theater was showing a two-reel film about Bonnie and Clyde when several women appeared and tore down posters and photos in the lobby. When the posters and photos were replaced the women again appeared, but the second time police were present and Mrs. Barrow was arrested and taken to police headquarters. After she apologized, she was released and apparently the incident was dropped.

Despite the desire to protect the memory of Bonnie and Clyde, *Fugitives: The Story of Clyde Barrow and Bonnie Parker* provides a first hand account and look behind the scenes of Bonnie and Clyde's crime spree. Surprisingly the book does not attempt to sugarcoat their exploits. It also helps to connect the dots as law enforcement chased the pair across the country.

Researchers are skeptical of much of the material in *Fugitives: The Story of Clyde Barrow and Bonnie Parker*. Many believe some names were changed to protect surviving family members, there are also instances when Mrs. Parker and Nell Cowan attempt to point blame for some of the more serious crimes at other members of the Barrow-Parker gang.

There is also a belief that Jan Fortune attempted to write a book that would appeal to readers and may have taken some jouranlistic liberties in portraying the story of Bonnie and Clyde.

However, despite these shortcomings, the book is a good read and does contain letters, diary entries and other information that might not otherwise have been made available to the public.

Foreward

There may be readers who will hesitate to open this volume, thinking that it is a vindication of Bonnie Parker and Clyde Barrow as persons who were more sinned against than sinning. Such people need have no fear. Within these pages you will find nothing to predicate such a fact. We feel that their life story, as set down here, is the greatest indictment known to modern times against a life of crime.

There is nothing in these pages which would attract any normal person to the life of an outlaw. The two years which Bonnie and Clyde spent as fugitives, hunted by officers from all over the Southwest, were the most horrible years ever spent by two young people. They were on the road constantly; they lived from hand to mouth; they never knew the happiness of safety and security; they had no home and rarely enough money.

Never for one instant did they experience a joy or a thrill which could possibly compensate them for the living hell which made up their lives. In- the last accounting, all they had left in life was each other and the pleasure of occasionally sneaking home to see their people. There never was a time, after the chase began, when they would not have traded places with the poorest and humblest couple on earth if they could have had peace and ordinary happiness.

They trusted but few fellow beings and even here as always that trust was betrayed. Bonnie and Clyde were betrayed by one they considered a friend. This was also true of Jesse James, of Cole Younger, of Pancho Villa, of John Dillinger, of Machine Gun Kelly. It will always be true of those who kill and steal and prey upon decent law-abiding society.

There was only one thing Bonnie and Clyde possessed which the above mentioned did not own: Clyde and Bonnie had a love which bound them together in life and went with them to their graves. We believe that no two people ever loved more devotedly, more sincerely, and more lastingly than Clyde Barrow and Bonnie Parker. This love was all they had to set them apart from others of their kind; and it was not enough. This recital of their life histories is put down as they told it to us, and from sources we consider reliable. Any discrepancies are not, therefore, of our making. We have told it as we learned it, except for some fictitious names here and there, used in order to avoid trouble for others.

The story of Bonnie and Clyde is offered to the reading public as a thrilling story of the exciting and hectic experiences of two youths who were misfits in society. It proves that crime never pays, and that indeed "the wages of sin is death."

FUGITIVES
The Story of Bonnie and Clyde

Nell Begins the Story

Millions of words have been written about Clyde Barrow and Bonnie Parker, who were shot to death by officers of the law near Arcadia, Louisiana, May 23, 1934. All over the world the reading public has been kept fully informed concerning the many crimes which they committed or were supposed to have committed. Reams of paper have been covered with their doings,— the sort of clothes Clyde wore, the way he drove, his ruthlessness, his daring; columns have been devoted to Bonnie's yellow hair, her painted toenails, her cigar-smoking proclivities, and her defiance of law and order.

But there has never yet been a story written which really told the truth about Clyde and Bonnie; never an account which showed them as they were; never an insight into their lives and characters as human beings. They were monsters, they were outlaws, they did unspeakable things. So said the press, so averred the law. The law and the press were both undoubtedly right.

There was another side to the story; another angle which only we, who loved them and suffered untold worry and torment for them, could possibly know. And during the

two years when the pair were being hunted down by officers, we, as kinsmen, had little to say for publication, which
was only natural under the circumstances. We dared not
talk. When the end of the trail had been reached for them
both, there was little need of talking. Talking would have
done no good, for the morbidly curious who fought their
way into the funeral homes to view all that was left of the
bodies of these two young people, were not interested in
anything except the gruesome and horrible facts, of which
there were plenty to satisfy everybody.

Now that the tumult and shouting has died away in some
measure, and the Barrows and the Parkers, released from
the hideous strain of two years waiting for what came during May, 1934, are beginning to live normal lives again, I
feel that I owe it to my brother, Clyde, and to the woman
whom he loved, Bonnie Parker, to present them before the
world as we knew them.

Not in extenuation, for of course there is no extenuation.
But as human beings who through circumstances became
involved in a life from which there was no going back; on a
road that knew no turning; as human beings who, strange
as it may seem, had their own code of morals, loyalties and
loves, and who lived and died by this code — I am almost
tempted to say that they died because of it. But let me tell
you the story and you shall be the judge.

My first childish memory, outstanding among other
memories, is of my little brother, Clyde. We were a large
family — there were eight of us children — and Clyde was
third from the youngest. I came next, and my brother Buck

was the next oldest after me. Clyde was born March 24, 1909.

The older children are a little hazy in my mind during that period, because they were so much older, and Clyde and I had very little companionship with the younger ones because we went away early in life to visit with relatives.

We lived on a farm at Teleco, Texas — just poor tenant farmers, who rarely ever had enough to eat, scanty clothes, and very few pleasures. My father, rather a silent man, with no education — he could neither read nor write — worked hard in the fields all day, coming in at night worn and weary. He had a single track mind and plodded wearily from year to year, never getting anywhere. My mother, with so many babies on hand, had little time for anything else except house work. I suppose we weren't a very happy family. I remember that all my good times were connected with my little brother, Clyde.

I was five when Clyde was born, and I loved him devotedly from the instant that my mother first allowed me to sit beside her bed in a rawhide bottom chair and hold him in my arms. We had named him Clyde Chestnut Barrow. Just where the newspapers got the name of Clyde Champion I don't know, for his middle name was Chestnut and it matched his hair as he grew older. The first time I saw Clyde he had cotton colored hair, dark brown eyes, and cheeks rosy as apples. He laughed a lot, even when a baby. I used to sit and hold him and squeeze him. It seemed to me that I loved him so much I couldn't squeeze him enough. Every day I squeezed a little harder, and he seemed to thrive and grow on it, kicking and squealing with delight.

There is a particular and poignant memory of a morning when Clyde was six months old. I had another squeezing spell. I gathered him up in my arms when my mother wasn't looking and squeezed with all my strength. But instead of the usual crow of delight, Clyde gurgled uncertainly, turned a sickly blue around the mouth, and when I set him back down on the floor, he promptly toppled over and lay there, very still and limp. I shook him, I rubbed him, I pulled him around and still he didn't move. Then I began to yell bloody murder, and my mother came running, took one look at the lifeless form and grabbed him up and dashed out the door.

We lived three miles from town, and our nearest neighbor was half a mile away up a hill. My mother was headed for the neighbor and aid. Terror fairly surged over me as I tagged along after her, holding to her skirts. Not terror for baby Clyde, but terror for little Nell Barrow, who was undoubtedly going to get the spanking of a lifetime whenever her mother got around to it. All the way up the hill I remember hanging onto her skirts and howling at the top of my lungs:

"I didn't go to do it, mama, I didn't go to do it!"

As it turned out, I never got the spanking though, for it was three hours before Clyde showed any signs of life, and three days before he was able to move around again normally. By that time my mother had gone through so much worry and suffering that spanking the cause of it all was the last thing in her mind.

Now that I look back, I don't remember ever getting any spankings. I don't remember that the boys got spanked either, though we certainly all needed it. My mother had a quick temper, too, and so did my father, but they simply didn't punish us, that's all. Maybe spankings would have been the thing Clyde and Buck needed; I don't know. Maybe spankings wouldn't have made any difference in the way they turned out, after all. There's never any way of telling when years have passed and things are over and done.

From the day I almost killed him there was a peculiar kinship between Clyde and me, which time never broke, and adversity and sorrow did not change. We were constant companions, despite the difference in our ages. We shared our joys, our troubles, our hopes and ambitions. I almost killed him another time, when he was four, but he never held it against me.

My two cousins and I had slipped off to the creek to go swimming, and Clyde tagged along. We weren't watching him carefully, for we were engrossed in our own fun. A threshing about in the water aroused us, and we discovered Clyde going under. There certainly was a scramble as the life-saving crew mobilized for action, but Clyde was perfectly limp by the time we got him on the bank. We knew nothing whatever of modern resuscitation methods, but we had enough sense to roll him back and forth on a bed of leaves and pump his arms around till he began to show signs of life. When he finally came to, we held solemn council and agreed to keep his drowning a secret among us. Clyde was very sporty about the matter. He agreed to keep it secret too. Someway, we just had the feeling that we'd all be better off if we didn't say anything about the matter when we got home.

By the time Clyde was six, he knew just what he was going to be: A hero like William S. Hart, who was the big screen menace at that time. We used to save our pennies so we could walk the three miles into town to the picture show, and sometimes if it was a very good one, we'd sit through it three or four times while our parents and the neighbors scoured the country for us.

Clyde loved guns from the time I can remember, and always played with them. Toy guns, if he could get them; if not, he'd use a stick for a gun. He was never afraid of anything, even as a baby. I remember when he was scarcely five that he disappeared from home one day before noon. We looked everywhere, — under the beds, under the house, and in the barns. We called in the neighbors; we dragged the well and the creek. As the afternoon wore on, mother was frantic, and my father, called in from the fields to join in the search, was for once moved out of his stoical calm. Such a little fellow to be lost — only five! He might be anywhere, injured, dying, dead. I cried while we hunted, and I cried with a clear conscience. For once, whatever had happened to Clyde, I hadn't done it.

It was almost dark when a wagon drove up to the house and the diminutive adventurer descended with all the aplomb and poise of a seasoned traveller. He said to his weeping and frantic family, using a lordly gesture: "Shucks! A man gave me some pennies and I couldn't spend 'em till

I got to town, could I? So I des walked in." He didn't get a spanking that time, either. We were too relieved to have him safely home again.

Although I was five years his senior, when we played, Clyde was the leader. He was Jesse James, or Cole Younger, or Buffalo Bill, or William S. Hart. He toted guns and shot from the hip with deadly aim, and cowards and redskins always bit the dust in the most approved fashion. It was up to me to be the cowards and the redskins. Many and bitter were the fights we had because I was never allowed to be Jesse James. But Clyde was going to be the big shot if we played, and if I kicked about it, we didn't play. It was very dull when Clyde refused to play, therefore I went on being cowards and redskins.

Clyde played hooky from school and I'd play hooky with him. Neither of us ever liked school, but until Clyde came along to take the lead, I'd gone to school because I thought I had to. Clyde had other ideas; we played hooky. Many a day we've taken our lunch and slipped away in the woods and stayed till school was out, building miniature fortresses out of sand, manning the tops of them with Indians made of corn cobs, and shooting them down without mercy when they offered resistance. I don't believe Texas had compulsory education at this time, and if so, it wasn't compulsory where we were living. No teacher ever reported our absence to our parents. I imagine they simply heaved sighs of relief that there were two less to devil them, and let it go at that.

We had few amusements, as I have said, except of our making, but Clyde had a fertile mind. He could always think up something interesting to do. He used to get out in the pasture and ride the calves till they could hardly totter. Mother didn't kick about that, but when he started riding her milk cows to and from the pasture at a gallop, there was a row. The day he let the fattening hogs out and rode them, there was a terrible row.

We were a stormy family, but loyal to each other. We had plenty of rows and fights among ourselves, but any attack from the outside, either in school or elsewhere, showed us presenting a solid front to the world and ready to whip anybody, no matter how many nor how big. We grew up that way. We all loved each other devotedly, but Clyde loved me and my mother the best. In fact, Clyde's love for his mother, even in his last desperate days, was subject for much newspaper comment. At one time before his death, officers arrested my mother and spirited her away from Dallas with a lot of newspaper publicity which went out all over the state. This was done solely in order to entice Clyde back home because he had said that if ever they harmed a hair of her head because of the things he'd done, he'd come in and kill them. But Clyde saw through the ruse, and a day later, mother was returned to us, safe and sound.

Though Buck wasn't as daring as Clyde, both Clyde and Buck rode wild horses whenever they could find one, and generally behaved like young dare devils. Buck was always slow, easy going, didn't like to work, and never cared for guns. He loved cock fights, and was always getting chickens and starting something. Sometimes, if there weren't any good fighters on our farm, Buck wasn't above lifting good fighters from surrounding farms, which is where, I suppose, the story got started that Clyde's first offence against the law was stealing chickens. Clyde never stole a chicken in his life, as police and juvenile records will show.

Our home conditions were very bad, as I know now. We lived in a small frame building of about three or four rooms, I don't recall the exact size, except that many of us slept on the floor. We had to work in the fields, chopping cotton, hoeing corn, doing whatever was necessary, as soon as we were able. I don't recall that we minded it so much because we didn't know any better. I remember only that Clyde had a quick temper, and would flare up and say things when he got mad. Then, when he cooled down, he was always exceedingly sorry he'd been so bad, and would try to do everything in his power to redeem himself and get us to laughing again.

When Clyde was six and I was eleven years old, we began spending a great deal of time with my father's brother, who lived on a farm near Corsicana. This uncle was crazy about both of us. We liked him and his home because he had children about our ages. Also, this uncle was very easygoing, and he didn't see why children should be made to go to school if they didn't want to, and he didn't send us. We worked on his farm some, hunted some, and played a lot. Our visits with him usually lasted about three months; then we'd have to go back home. We never stayed at home long at a time. At the first chance, we'd go back to the Corsicana uncle and freedom. This went on three years, Clyde and I having a grand time on this visiting schedule, but learning very little.

When I was fourteen and Clyde nine, we went to visit on a ranch at Mabank, Texas, with another uncle. Here we went to a rural community school situated between Mabank and Trinidad. Things weren't as easy here because this uncle wasn't as lax about such little matters as learning how to spell and do sums. He made us go to school. However, after school we had the chance to ride horseback after the cattle, and we liked that. I remember particularly on this ranch I helped Clyde steal some sausage — my first and last adventure into crime — but at the time we felt we were thoroughly justified.

This uncle's wife was very stingy. Every fall when hog killing time came around she would put by in the smoke house all of the delectable pieces of fresh killed meat, and fry up tons of sausage and pack them in their own grease. The hams and shoulders and bacon we never saw except on state occasions, but three times a day for month on end we were served re-heated sausage out of the fried sausage barrel. Finally Clyde said he couldn't eat another sausage, if he starved. We decided on drastic measures and stole the sausage. Since the place was simply alive with hunting dogs, hound dogs, watch dogs, and just plain dogs, we lured them out behind the smoke house and fed them sausage till they were puffed up like balloons and walked funny. This necessity measure still didn't do away with all the sausage for even a dog's capacity is limited. We were still eating some of it when we left and went to live with an uncle at Kerens. In fact, the sausage was one of the reasons that we moved.

But the Kerens uncle meant to get his money's worth out of us. He was more than strict, and he certainly made us work. We had to get up hours before dawn to go to the field or help with the stock. I remember how Clyde complained bitterly more than once that he was tired of going to work before the dew was off the ground, because by sun-up his clothes were always dripping wet. This Kerens business didn't last very long.

Our parents gave up farming in 1922, and moved to Dallas. I was seventeen and Clyde was twelve, and we decided to come to Dallas too. I found a job and went to live in town with a friend. Clyde left me for the first time since he was born, and went to live with my mother and father in West Dallas. Here he attended his last school, the Cedar Valley School. He was in the fifth grade. When he was sixteen, he stopped school and got a job with the Exline-Exline Co. He worked variously with several firms during this time, including the Nu-Grape Co., the Western Union as messenger — he was here six months — and finally at Proctor and Gamble's.

One of the first things Clyde bought from his earnings was a stripped down speedster, quite an old model, for which he paid $50. He was inordinately proud of it and got quite a kick out of running around in it. I married about this time and moved into a cottage over on Pear Street in South Dallas. Clyde promptly drove his speedster over and moved in with us.

I was very glad to have him, for my husband played in

an orchestra and was away from home a lot. I was lonesome, but Clyde's coming changed all that and things became lively right away. We enjoyed each other with perfect understanding and perfect comradeship. Clyde had grown into a very handsome boy. He had always been tremendously fond of me, and so thoroughly lovable and full of fun that he was a joy to have in the house. We pranked together like two kids.

Clyde was always very fond of music. When a kid on the farm, he used to play the jew's-harp and sing. I remember when he was eleven he went down to Mexia during the oil boom and held a job watching the oil rigs at night. During the long tedious evenings, he used to play and sing for the roughnecks and roustabouts, and they paid him for it, as grown people often pay precocious children. Clyde still wanted to be a musician when he came to live with us, and he took advantage of the fact that my husband owned a saxophone. Clyde started learning to play the saxophone, and the air up and down Pear Street was split with harsh, discordant sounds for many weeks till I've no doubt the neighbors were often on the verge of turning us in for disturbing the peace. But Clyde loved his saxophone playing and kept it up.

One day I came home from a visit and announced proudly to Clyde that I had learned to play the ukulele. At that time the ukulele was a very fashionable instrument, and almost everybody played one, or tried to. They were selling for $1.98, and the instant I told Clyde that I was an accomplished "uke" performer, his face brightened like a full moon: "If you can play it, so can I," he exclaimed. "Let's buy a 'uke' right now, Sis!"

Our combined finances amounted to $1.50. We went through the house like a fine tooth comb, looking for extra pennies, and finally, after a lengthy search, we got together the additional 48 cents. But we had no carfare. Clyde wasn't to be balked by a little thing like that. He walked to town, a matter of about eight miles for the round trip, and returned several hours later triumphantly bearing the "uke."

Here again we hit a snag. Neither of us knew how to tune it, and this was indeed a catastrophe after all our efforts. We located ten cents more, borrowing four from a neighbor, and then ordered two ice cream cones from the drug store. The instant the colored delivery boy brought them, Clyde, waiting on the front steps, pounced on him.

"Ike, can you tune a ukulele?" Clyde demanded.

"Sho kin, Mistah Clyde," the negro replied, and reached for it. Ike tuned the "uke." Then Clyde made him sit down on the front steps and play *Saint Louis Blues* till the pharmacy telephoned to know what had become of their delivery boy. After that, Clyde and I "uked" for weeks, and sang to our own accompaniments proudly. Whenever the thing got out of tune, we ordered two ice cream cones from the drug store and made Ike tune it again.

It was spring, and Clyde was beginning to notice girls. He began to be a very careful dresser, and to want his clothes just so. He took pains to shave every day, to keep his hair cut precisely, and to care for his fingernails. These were habits he acquired early and never lost as long as he lived.

He was nearly always immaculate, even after days spent on the road, fleeing from the law.

One lovely spring day Clyde came in at noon from Proctor and Gamble's. He had his wrist tied up, and when I asked him in concern what was the matter, he explained patiently and sweetly that he had sprained it and had to knock off work. Ten minutes later I found him putting on a tie before the mirror in his room, using one wrist as easily as the other. He was also whistling gaily.

"Listen here, Clyde Barrow," I said severely, "you tell me the truth. There's not a thing in the world the matter with your wrist, is there, now?"

He grinned in the mirror at me, that boyish, lovable grin, and then winked. "Not a thing," he confessed gaily. "It was just too swell a day to stay in and work, that's all. You know how it is, Sis." Then he swung around and hugged me, and went back to tying his tie.

I scolded him, but it was half-hearted scolding, for I did know how it was. I knew too, how Clyde loved a good time and how few good times he'd had when growing up. I didn't scold him hard. I even fixed his tie a little better for him. Then he backed his rattle trap car down the driveway and went bumping off down Pear Street in the spring sunshine.

That night marked the first time Clyde ever got into any sort of trouble with the officers of the law. He was rather late coming in, and I heard the car hit the drive going about forty, dash down toward the garage and bump into the porch with a bang. Then suddenly there was Clyde in the kitchen door, looking flustered and nervous. "Sis," he whispered to me, "if anybody comes here and asks you who drove that car tonight, don't you tell them — hear?"

I wasn't a bit scared. I had no premonition that this was the beginning of the long trail that was to end in death. I just laughed and said: "Now, what in the world have you been up to, Clyde?"

He laughed too, the color coming into his face again. "I was just speeding a little," he confessed. "It's so much fun to go fast," he rushed on when he saw my face sober. "The smart old cops whistled at me, so I put on all I had and ran for it."

"But, Clyde, you should have stopped," I told him. "They'd just have scolded you if you'd stopped. It's running away that gets you in bad."

His face clouded, grew sullen. "I hate rows," he muttered. "It's easier to run away."

I know now that this was the very beginning right there. Clyde hated rows and running away was easier than staying and trying to explain, or taking his medicine. Clyde was to run away consistently the rest of his life. Later, as a criminal, when he could not run away, he kidnapped officers or shot his way out. I had no way of knowing this at that time, and if I had known, could I have changed him any? I don't think so. He was made the way he was and nobody could have changed him except himself. The time was to come, however, when because of Bonnie Parker, Clyde would have liked to have changed, but by then it was too late, forever and ever.

So when he begged me ingratiatingly this spring night:

"You wont tell on me when they come, will you, Sis?" I promised that I wouldn't. And I never broke that promise. I never told on him about anything till the day he died.

But the cops didn't come that night. They didn't come till much later when Clyde had his first love affair. And when they came that time, Clyde ran away again.

Clyde's first romance began in the fall of 1925. He met Anne B., who was a student of Forest Avenue High School in Dallas. Clyde's delightful personality and his ability to make people like him was attested over and over by the fact that although he had almost no education and no background, the most respectable and educated people were his friends, and the nicest girls fell in love with him.

This was true of all three of his major love affairs. It began with Anne B., who graduated while still going with Clyde, directly against her mother's wishes; it included Gladys, who lived with him in Dallas as his wife for almost a year; and it ended with Bonnie Parker who was the prize pupil in the Cement City High School. All three of these girls had more than ordinary educations. All three had been reared in homes of middle class culture and refinement, with ideals, morals, and conventions drilled into them from birth. They loved him devotedly, against parental objections, against public opinion, and undoubtedly against their own better judgments. That was the sort of boy Clyde was; that was why he could always get by with his escapades. When these escapades became offences against the state, grew into crimes, and ended in outlawry and banditry, there were still those of us who loved him and stuck by him, even while shuddering at every fresh newspaper story.

Another incongruous thing about Clyde at this period, considering his later record, was that he was never fired from a job, that he liked to work — (the juvenile court records have this fact written into their papers) — and that all his employers liked him. More than that, he had a splendid credit rating and could buy anything he wanted on it. He paid his bills. He bought Anne B. a wrist watch which she still has, some expensive leather luggage, an onyx ring, a diamond engagement ring and a wedding ring. I wear the engagement ring now.

Clyde was working at Proctor and Gamble's when he met Anne. Her brother met Clyde and liked him — liked him so much, in fact, that he brought him home and introduced him to his sister. Clyde fell desperately in love. He was only sixteen and love hit him hard. He regaled me by the hour concerning the beauties and superlative qualities of this girl, and she was indeed all the things he said she was.

He went with Anne all winter. He had changed jobs now, going to the A. and K. Auto Top Works, where he received a better salary. Clyde worked well and conscientiously. He was going to marry Anne just as soon as she finished school. At that time her parents made no objection, for Clyde had never yet had any dealing with the law (except for truancy from Cedar Valley School), and some minor juvenile offences that were not known.

Despite the many stories which describe him as small and undersized, with a weak chin and shifty eye, I can only produce pictures to prove that he was very handsome and quite well-built, and state the fact that his friends were many and numerous, and equally divided between both sexes. Clyde was not a ladies' man; he was just an ordinary young boy with more good looks and personality than the average, and everybody who knew him, liked him. Although they were not sanctioning such an early wedding, even Anne's parents liked him. They felt that Clyde and Anne should wait a few years, at least. Clyde had no such intentions, as the purchase of the wedding ring shows.

It was not till the spring of 1926 that Clyde got into his first trouble, and that, as I have said, was because of a girl — Anne, in fact. They had a quarrel, during which Clyde said some very nasty things, and Anne got up and marched off to San Augustine to visit with an aunt, and left Clyde to think matters over. I have stated elsewhere that Clyde had a hot temper and flew off the handle easily. Also, he was very headstrong, and wanted to boss people whom he loved. He had tried this on Anne and it hadn't worked.

No sooner was she out of town than Clyde was sorry and dying to ask forgiveness. He had a brilliant idea: He would go to San Augustine. Since his speedster had fallen apart long ago, and had been sold for junk, he would rent a car and bring Anne back. In order to be doubly armed against refusal, he would take Anne's mother along with him. So he went down to Nichols Bros, and rented a car, but he only hired it for the afternoon. Just why he didn't hire it for a day, I'm sure, was a matter of finances. If they'd known he was taking the car to San Augustine, they'd have made him put up a pretty stiff deposit, and I'm sure he didn't have it.

Then he drove out to Anne's house and asked Mrs. B. if she would like to visit with her kinsfolk in San Augustine. It seemed that Mrs. B. would. Naturally, she knew nothing about the peculiar car arrangement. If she had, I'm sure she'd have stayed home rather than ride in it.

At San Augustine, Anne and Clyde made up immediately. Everything was rosy; Clyde loved Anne and Anne loved Clyde; nothing was ever to separate them again. So happy were they that Clyde overlooked the fact that the car should be returned to Dallas with all haste. Instead, he stayed two days, waiting for Mrs. B. to get her visit out.

Back in Dallas the rent car people began to be worried about the prolonged absence of their automobile. They telephoned Clyde's place of business, then his home, and learned that he had gone to the B.'s They were informed that Mrs. B. and Clyde were both in San Augustine. The rest was easy. Officers at San Augustine were notified, and on the afternoon of the second day, they appeared at the farmhouse in San Augustine looking for the car and for Clyde.

Here Clyde made another big mistake. If he had met the officers, told his story simply and convincingly, and offered to make good the rental on the car, I'm sure nothing would have come of it. People the world over are sympathetic with young love, and Clyde was just seventeen that spring. But he didn't like rows, and it was easier to run away. When the officers came, he ran. He ran through a cornfield, and when they called "Halt!" he ran the harder. Two shots fired after the retreating figure, dodging in and out among the cornstalks, did nothing to retard his pace. He ran and ran, till he passed the fields and hid in the woods. Here he stayed till night came, then slipped back to the farm house. Anne prevailed on her aunt for the use of the family car and drove Clyde to Broadus to catch the Dallas train. Clyde's reception was rather cool, and he was speeded on his way without invitation to return. Only Anne was sweet and kind to him.

She bade him a tearful farewell as she left him in Broadus, and came back to hear her mother speak her mind forcefully about Clyde Barrow. Mrs. B. was packing to go home, and she said as she packed, that the engagement was over, as far as Anne was concerned, and that was that.

In the meantime, in Broadus waiting for the train, Clyde had had time for thought. He realized that he hadn't behaved as a gentleman should where his girl's mother was concerned. He had brought her down to San Augustine, and then left her with no way to get back home except the train. She'd likely never forgive him for that, and it looked as if he was in bad enough without this added handicap. He figured that the least he could do would be to get a car somewhere — anywhere — and go back for Anne and her mother and drive them home. He left the station and went looking for a car to "borrow" — that was the phrase he used when telling me the story — and drove back in it to San Augustine. But Mrs. B. and her daughter had already gone.

Disconsolately, Clyde started back to Dallas in the stolen car, his idea being to drive it in and leave it on the streets somewhere so that officers might pick it up and return it to the owner. But he had not gone far till a car came toward him, slowed up and stopped. Fear seized Clyde. He shut off the engine, jumped into the ditch, and ran away again. Looking back, he discovered that it wasn't officers of the law, coming to bring him to justice, but just a car full of drunken negroes. However, the scare had been too much for him. He got out on the highway and started hitch-hiking, and thus came home. He went out to my mother's when he got back. He was afraid to face me, because he knew I'd get the truth out of him and give him Hail Columbia!

Strangely enough, no one ever did find out that Clyde took the car at Broadus, and when the auto rent matter came up, Clyde was excused because he was such a kid and it was his first offence. I was angry about the whole affair, but my sympathies were all with Clyde, of course. I felt that it was just a childish prank any boy might play when young and in love, and I didn't put the proper significance to it, or talk to him as I should have. It seemed rather funny — his logic and reasoning during the whole affair.

Neither did I take too seriously the events which occurred just before Christmas of that year. Buck took all the blame and Buck was the one I bawled out. We hadn't much money, of course, and Buck wanted some cash for the holidays. I'll never know whether or not Clyde really had anything to do with this. All I do know is that Buck had the back of the car full of turkeys, and Clyde was with him when the officers caught them. They were arrested and taken to jail. Here Buck assumed all the blame and got a week's sentence. Clyde was allowed to go.

Everything would have been all right if it hadn't been that this made Clyde's second offence against the law, and that Buck, who was notorious for stealing, had been up several times previous to this for petty thievery. The officers began classing the Barrow boys together, and every time Buck did something, they took Clyde down as a matter of course, even though they turned him loose each time. This began to make Clyde resentful of the law, and disgusted with their methods. He complained to me several times that just because Buck stole was no sign he did, and that he wished the smart cops would realize the fact.

Clyde was still working, but he was rather choosey about his jobs and had a good opinion of his own ability. This characteristic is not objectionable, provided one can carry through and deliver the goods, which he seemed to be doing at this period. I remember that he was out of work for a few weeks before Christmas and went to the Palace Theater as an usher. When he discovered that the salary was only $12 a week, he came home in high dudgeon and said they could take their puny job and go to the lower regions with it.

After Christmas Clyde went to work for the United Glass and Mirror Co. where he worked two years, and here he built church windows for many Dallas churches. He also made lovely mirrors, and presented some to Anne with her name on them. Anne's dates with him were growing fewer and fewer, and were always under cover because of violent parental objection concerning young Mr. Barrow, who had

had too many brushes with the law to suit Anne's folks as a son-in-law.

The affair finally died a natural death, and Clyde, on a visit to Wichita Falls, met and fell in love with a beautiful girl named Gladys. Early in his love affair with Anne, he had had his arm tattooed with her name. Now he put Gladys' name on the other arm. There was no arm left for Bonnie's name, when she finally came along, but it wasn't necessary, for Bonnie's name was written on his heart.

Clyde came home from Wichita Falls, bringing Gladys with him, and announced to me that they were married. It seemed a rather jumped-up wedding to me — the whole thing seemed hasty — but I took his word for it that Gladys was everything in the world. He rented light house keeping rooms over on Liberty Street, set up his first home, and asked me over to visit with him and Gladys.

She was a likable person, very slim and pretty, and we got along very well. Where Clyde was concerned I had uncanny powers of discernment. It wasn't long before I began to sense that things weren't going exactly right. Gladys wanted too many things which Clyde's salary at the United Glass Company didn't cover. She wanted a lot of clothes, a watch, money for good times, and a car. When these things were not all forthcoming, she was very disagreeable. Clyde began to be restless and dissatisfied with life and his job.

About this time my husband and I came to the parting of the ways. I left him, and at Clyde's urgent request, I moved in with the newly-weds. There were lots of scenes between them, and many bitter words spoken. Besides the endless bickering over money, Gladys was constantly at him about Anne's name on his arm. She was furiously jealous of Anne, and although she didn't know her, was always making some remark about her. Clyde would answer back, and the fur would fly. When he'd make her shut up about Anne, the row for a car or money would start.

He went to Oklahoma and stole a car, as I learned later. When he came home, he took it over to a garage on the West Dallas pike, and told me he'd be there all day working, and for me to come over. We always liked being together better when Gladys wasn't around. I drove my car over and hunted Clyde up around noon. When I reached the garage, I found Clyde filing the numbers off the engine — a rather unusual proceedure that didn't look right to me. I asked him whose car it was and where he'd gotten it. He replied, both dimples working, that it belonged to a friend, and that he was overhauling it.

"Mighty funny overhauling," I stated determinedly. "You stole this car, Clyde. You know you stole it."

He just roared with laughter, denied the accusation as of no importance, and started pouring lye over the hood to take the paint off. I was certain the car was stolen by then, and we had a big row over it, during which Clyde said some very nasty things, and accused me of being suspicious, disloyal, and having a dirty mind. I refused to speak to him and his face was blazing with anger. I drove home and packed my clothes and moved over to mama's.

Just a few weeks later, Gladys left him and went back to Wichita Falls. Whether she moved because she found out about the car, and wouldn't stand for it, or whether she left because they had another big row over Anne B., I don't know. I found out that they hadn't really been married. Clyde sold the stolen car, and to this day, there's never been an inquiry about it which connected Clyde with its theft.

Clyde didn't come home after Gladys left him. Instead he went to live with a boy named Frank Clause and if I'd had the gift of second sight, or been able to read the future, I'd have killed Clyde rather than let him go with Frank Clause. Frank had a police record already, and was really a bad egg. He was fairly nice looking, and as he seemed to be a nice boy, I didn't suspect anything for a while, or dream the sort of life Clyde was being drawn into.

About this time I got a job again and moved in town to live in an apartment with another girl. One night, very late, Frank Clause and Clyde came by the house and got me out of bed. They had four bricks of ice cream, a handful of pocket knives, some hot water bottles, and a lot of other stuff which they spread out on the kitchen table. They got out bowls and dished up the ice cream, and when I demanded to know where they had found all this junk, Clyde told me the most marvelous lie I ever listened to. He said there had been a drug store fire out in Oak Cliff, and he and Frank just happened to be driving past and had seen people throwing all sorts of things out in the street, and as every body else was doing the same thing, they had stopped and helped themselves.

Naturally, I didn't believe a word of it and I said so. Again we had a big row, and Clyde left in a huff. I was worried to death about him by now. I had found out that he had quit his job since going to live with Frank Clause, and something warned me that things weren't going right. But still I wouldn't believe that he would do anything really criminal himself. I just wouldn't believe that.

It was after this drug store affair that Clyde, Frank Clause, Buck, and a new boy from Houston were arrested by the officers for hanging around the offices of the Buell Lumber Co. They were carried to jail and held for questioning on suspicion that they had been planning to stick up the Buell Lumber Co.

I don't remember how they got out of it —somebody must have made bond for them, or something — but anyhow, I know all four of them came out to my mother's house that day and stayed the rest of the day and spent the night there, because I was there when they arrived, and I was also there the next morning when the police came after them again.

The instant the boys heard the officers talking to my mother, they all made a run for it. One of them went under the house and hid; Buck fell, going out the back door, and sprained his ankle; Frank and Clyde made for the open spaces, but when the officers shot at them, they came back. I remember Clyde was crying when he came to where my mother was in the kitchen: "Gosh, mama," he sniffed, "I've just got out of that awful place — I can't go back down there — honest, I can't!"

I was boiling mad and I spoke my mind to those cops, right and left. "They couldn't have done anything since you let them out of jail," I stormed. "They've been right here the whole time. How do you expect boys to do any better when you hound them all the time? You ought to be ashamed, that's what!" I raved and railed, for Clyde's tears had touched me. After all, he was hardly eighteen; he was still just a little boy, and he was crying and I was his sister. Naturally, my mind wasn't functioning very well about law and order.

The officers didn't get mad when I spouted off. They just grinned and let me have my say. They told me that other things had come up which necessitated further questioning of the boys. For one thing, they'd like to know just where Clyde got that yellow Buick roadster parked out in the yard? I said that was my car and Clyde had nothing to do with it. They said they were taking it along, just the same, with the boys. At that, I marched out and climbed in, still as mad as a wet hen, and announced that if that car went, I was driving it. I knew the car wasn't "hot" as the law called it. I happened to know that Clyde bought it and paid for it; I knew the people he purchased it from, and I didn't intend to let the officers take it away from him.

Off we went, I driving and the cop sitting up beside me having trouble keeping his face straight, for I was still sputtering like a fire cracker. Just for meanness I ran through two red lights with that cop, but he didn't say a word. The other boy wasn't along. He was still under the house and they didn't get him that trip, but they had Clyde, and I meant to help him out, even if I should get in jail myself. I didn't realize how futile my gesture was till later.

Down at the station the chief looked me over when I

marched in, still hopping mad, and asked me just where I bought that car? I gave him the desired information. They wanted to know if I hadn't been letting Clyde use it a lot. I said, "Sure — of course — and so what?"

"Nothing," he replied, looking at me, "only you might as well stop trying to lie for him. He's already told us that the car is his, and the reason we're interested in it is because there's been a lot of safe cracking going on in Lufkin and Hillsboro, and every time a job is pulled, that yellow road-ster has been in town, that's all."

I wouldn't believe him at first, but they kept hammering it into me. They said Clyde had been cracking safes for several months — ever since his friendship with Frank Clause. I could figure back. Frank had big ideas about how to get along in the world. I was heartbroken, and the officers sent me on back home to break the news to mother that Clyde was definitely a criminal. It wasn't a happy day.

Just how the boys got out of jail again I don't recall. Perhaps the officers couldn't prove anything, no matter what they knew. At any rate, they were out of jail again in a few days. Years later, Anne startled me by telling me that the last few months she went with Clyde he told her that he and some boys entered a place and stole the safe, a small one, and carried it out in the country during the night. Here they stayed till nearly daylight, trying to open it, but being new at the job of safe breaking, they were never successful, and finally had to leave it there. The police discovered it a few days later, intact. That was another thing they couldn't chalk up against Clyde because they didn't know it.

This scare about the safe robberies apparently didn't cool off Clyde any, because in just a few weeks after they were out of jail he, Buck, another fellow, and Sidney Albert Moore went to Henrietta and stole a car. They went to Denton where they robbed a garage. Here again they lifted the safe and got it into the car and started off. Clyde was driving, and even at this early age, his driving was reckless and daring. The officers sighted them and tried to whistle them down; Clyde put on his gas and made a corner on two wheels, ran into the curb, broke the front axle and threw Clyde out. When he hit the ground he kept on running.

He heard a shot as he ran, and a scream of pain from Buck, and thought surely they'd killed him, he said afterwards. After a night spent in the back alleys of Denton, he beat it for home, and he was a pretty scared boy when he got in. The papers stated that Buck received a flesh wound. Also, they were looking for a fourth man, unidentified, but Clyde laid low. Buck was sentenced to five years in the state penitentiary. This Denton affair happened in October, 1929. Buck began his sentence at Huntsville January 14, 1930. Sidney Moore drew a ten year sentence. Buck had again taken all the blame for the affair and done everything he could to keep Clyde clear from complicity in the Denton matter.

Buck's taking the blame for the Denton stick-up wasn't enough to get Clyde off, because there was a whole lot behind him that none of us knew about. He was wanted at Sherman and at Waco too. It wasn't long till they had Clyde behind the bars again. During this time, while he was still free, still apparently just a normal boy, full of fun, lovable, fond of a good time, he met Bonnie Parker, the girl who was to give him the last two years of her life with a devotion and a selfsacrificing love that surpasses my understanding, even now.

Bonnie was an adorable little thing, more like a doll than a girl. She had yellow hair that kinked all over her head like a baby's, the loveliest skin I've ever seen without a blemish on it, a regular cupid's bow of a mouth, and blue, blue eyes. Clyde always called her his "blue-eyed baby" or his "little blue-eyed girl." She had dimples that showed constantly when she talked, and she was so tiny; she was only four feet, ten inches tall, and weighed between eighty-five and ninety pounds. Her hands took a number five glove, and her feet a number three shoe. She was so full of the joy of living, she seemed to dance over the ground instead of walking; she always had a comeback for any wisecrack; her sense of humor was applied to herself as well as to the other fellow; she worked hard, lived at home, stayed in nights and never ran around; and, she simply adored and worshipped her mother. All in all, Bonnie Parker was the answer to a sister's prayer for a wife for a best loved brother. I hoped, when she found out about it, she'd overlook Clyde's police record, make a good boy out of him and stick to him.

She overlooked his past with a sympathy and a compassion that is evident only when a woman loves a man with all her heart and soul; and God knows she stuck by him till death came to them both. But, try though she did (her letters to him prove that she did try), she was never able to change him, nor to turn him aside from the path which he had chosen to follow. So seeing, after two years, the futility of her efforts, and faced with the alternative of living as a law abiding citizen without Clyde's presence and love, or of going with him on his career of crime which eventually led to murder, she chose to go with him, live with him and die with him. As I look back over the past, I realize that Bonnie's key crime was that she loved Clyde Barrow. . . .

Mrs. Parker Begins Bonnie's Story

It is far more difficult, I suspect, for a mother to write about her daughter than for a sister to write of her brother's life. In the first place, the viewpoint is bound to be different. Nell was always on equal footing with Clyde, because they were children together; he had no hidden secrets in his heart she couldn't share. It's different between parent and child, for there's always a wall; always hidden places, no matter how understanding a parent may strive to be. And for this reason, although the tie between Bonnie and myself was always very close, now and then I shall let her cousin, Bess, who was raised with her, relate incidents.

Bonnie was the middle child born to me. She first opened her eyes upon this world at the little town of Rowena, Texas, October 1, 1910. Hubert, whom we always called Buster, was two years older than she, and her baby sister, Billie, was born three years later. My husband was a brick layer, and we had the average home with the average conveniences. Our affiliations were with the Baptist Church of Rowena, and outside of church activities, socials, box suppers, and the like, we had very little social life.

Buster was a sober sort of youngster, and when Billie came, she was spoiled and petted by her grandmother and the rest of the kin. Bonnie was a bouncing ball of energy and laughter as soon as she was able to sit alone. She was a beautiful baby, with cotton colored curls, the bluest eyes you ever saw, and an impudent little red mouth. She was always into something from the time she could toddle, and kept the whole family on the run to get her out of her scrapes.

I recall as one of her earliest escapades, the plight she put Buster into one day at Sunday School. Buster was five and Bonnie three, and it was his job to take her to Sunday School every Sunday morning. He really was awfully proud of his little sister, and used to march off holding her by the hand, her curls shining in the sun and her little feet toddling along beside his longer steps, trying to keep up. This day seemed just like other Sundays when they left, but it wasn't when they got back, for Buster was in a towering rage. He marched into the house, Bonnie dancing impishly along behind him, and announced to all and sundry that he was "through with girls," and as far as his sister's religious education was concerned, somebody else in the family could see after it.

It turned out that at Sunday School each little tot had been asked up on the platform to sing a hymn, and when it came Bonnie's turn, she arose, mounted the stage proudly, resplendent in starched bows and ruffles, and sang *"He's A Devil In His Own Home Town"* in a singularly clear and piercing treble. Naturally, Buster was mortified to death, but Bonnie wasn't. She'd created a sensation and she had enjoyed it. No other song had caused the ripple of surprise that hers had caused. She failed to share Buster's mortification at all.

When Bonnie was four, my husband's brother came to

visit us and took keen delight in teaching baby Bonnie to swear at her father. My husband, though he would spank Buster for even a darn, thought Bonnie's swearing was just too cute, and would do nothing about it, so it was left to me to use the hair brush where it would do the most good.

In 1914, my husband died suddenly, and I was left with three small children and the problem of providing for them. My mother, who lived at Cement City near Dallas, offered me her home as my own. I moved to Dallas and got a job, of necessity leaving the children with her while I went out to work. It was here that Bonnie and my sister's daughter, Bess, came to make a team which caused us all a lot of inconvenience. For Bess was three years older than Bonnie, although small for her age, and between what she could think up and what came naturally to Bonnie, the households were generally in a stew from morning to night. My mother had to use hair brushes on Bonnie, while Bess' mother used slippers on Bess. They were the most lovable and adorable youngsters, for all their pranks, and we all adored them, even while spanking as hard as we could.

When Bonnie was six, she entered Cement City School, and proceeded to fight her way through it. She was always in a scrap of some sort, and would as soon jump on a boy twice her size as not. When things got too difficult, Bess would come to her rescue and the two of them mowed a wide row through school activities. But Bonnie learned fast and got on with her studies. She was never teacher's pet — she was too full of mischief to suit a teacher — but she was a precocious child, and always the one they chose to speak

pieces and sing songs, and otherwise show off when there
was need to put on a good front at school.

One of her chief delights was learning to act. An expression teacher came out from Dallas every week to teach
what we used to call "elocution," and Bonnie took to it like
a duck to water. She simply loved it, and in a short time,
she learned to imitate the people she knew, and often did
it, much to their embarrassment.

The teacher of expression, not having to put up with
Bonnie all day long, fell in love with what she termed "this
adorable child," and used to get my permission to bring
her into Dallas to spend the night with her. After Bonnie's
death I met this same teacher in the funeral home where
Bonnie's body lay, and she recalled the days of Bonnie's
childhood, and told me how her grandfather used to roll
the rugs back whenever she brought Bonnie home. Then,
on his all fours, he would romp and play for hours with her,
being a horse, a steamship, a monkey or a whole cage full of
lions, just as Bonnie demanded.

I remember once early in Bonnie's school days how she
ruined the Friday afternoon program given for the children's parents. Bonnie was playing the part of a pickaninny
on the stage with a lot of other children. She had smut on
her face and a stocking cap over her yellow hair. Before the
program started she had an argument with one of the boys
in her grade. Up on the stage with her, this youngster decided that a good way to get even with Bonnie would be to
jerk her stocking cap off and show the audience that after
all, it wasn't a negro, but that cotton headed little Parker

girl. So he jerked.

Bonnie was so outraged at thus being taken out of character before everybody that she began weeping tears of anger. The smut ran down onto her dress, and the tears made white streaks. The boy who was the cause of it all, snickered, and that was too much. Bonnie tore into him right before everybody. And at that, the audience just howled. Bonnie stopped at the sound of laughter. It gave her a new idea. Things weren't so bad, after all, apparently. People were being amused. She would amuse them further. She backed off and started turning somersaults and cartwheels right down the middle of the stage, and the program broke up in a riot.

Cousin Bess Relates

Being with Bonnie was always more fun than any other form of amusement, and we were kindred spirits from the minute I first laid eyes on her when she was four, and came to live with grandmother. Aunt Em (Mrs. Parker) was away all day at work, and grandmother had to take care of baby Billie, who was her pet, but Bonnie and I, after our work was done, would always slip off and plan our own fun, leaving Billie out of it if we could, because she'd tell grandmother if she found out.

I remember that Bonnie and I always took off our long winter underwear fully two months before we were supposed to do so, and hid it between the mattress and the feather beds. Once or twice we'd get caught, but on the whole we managed very nicely. Another thing we didn't like was the bags of asafetida grandma put around our necks, and we'd saw the string in two with a butcher knife. Billy used to beg us to get hers off too, but we wouldn't do it because we knew she'd tell who did it the minute grandma missed it, and we'd get a spanking.

Grandfather had a high raftered, old fashioned barn, and Bonnie and I, who had an urge at that time to be circus performers, would climb up in the loft and skin the cat on the rafters, twenty feet from the ground. Of course, we were constantly in danger of falling and breaking our fool necks, but that idea never occurred to us. We enjoyed ourselves thoroughly till an aunt who lived over the way, caught us at it. Then we got a pair of good spankings and orders to stay out of that barn.

The barn happened to be so situated that we couldn't get in at the door without this aunt seeing us, and if she saw us, we knew she'd tell. We were in a spot. But finally Bonnie found a hole on the far side where we could crawl through, shinny up a ladder and reach the hay loft without being seen, and continue our practicing for the circus careers without being caught.

Playing with fire was another strictly forbidden joy, but Bonnie and I managed this, too. We took some feed sacks and built us a wigwam behind the barn, close to the garden. Here we made a fire inside, safe from prying eyes, and roasted our potatoes, or whatever else we could obtain to eat. Provisions became increasingly difficult to secure. Grandmother couldn't be everywhere at once, but she was guardian of her pantry, don't mistake that, and suspected Bonnie and me on every occasion. I take the credit for the idea which got us more potatoes. We called Billie to us and sent her in to the front of the house to ask grandma for something; while thus engaged, we were able to sneak into the kitchen and lift potatoes for roasting.

We buried them in the ashes, and all was going well till we heard grandma's voice calling. She wanted something from the store. The fire was blazing pretty high in the wigwam at this moment, but we knew that we had better go. When we got back, the fire was out of control. It burned the wigwam, the potatoes, and caught the back fence on fire. Grandma was out there with a pan of water and a wet sack tied on a broom, fighting the fire. My mother and the other aunt and the neighbors were helping her. When the fire was out, the paddling we did get! We ate standing up for a week.

Bonnie and I decided we would be opera singers. We would climb on the pig pen at the coming of dusk, lift our heads toward the moon, and split the air with what we fondly hoped was music. This went on night after night during that summer. We once took some of grandpa's snuff when we were sent to bring it to him. Bonnie said: "You take some first, Bess, and see how it works." It worked swell. I was practically a new creature in a few minutes. Bonnie didn't follow my example. But the day we found grandpa's keg of green wine in the hayloft, Bonnie and I both indulged. The next thing I knew, there she lay as blue around the mouth as if she'd been eating bluing, and saying nothing.

Our well worked with a hand pump and it had to be primed in order to get it started. I'll never forget how the cold perspiration dripped off my knees while I pumped water to pour over Bonnie. I'd poured two buckets of water on her before the family caught on, but she was so sick that that was one time we didn't get spanked. Grandpa did move the wine, however.

Bonnie was scared to death of guns. Grandpa had one he kept under his pillow—a whopping big old fashioned pistol — and whenever we made the beds, I was always the one who had to reach under and lift it out gingerly and carry it at arm's length to the dresser. Once or twice Bonnie touched it without knowing it was there, and such screaming I never heard. I used to remember those days after Bonnie went away with Clyde, and wonder how she ever learned to handle guns, load for him, even fire them herself, for I never saw any one a bigger coward about them than she was when we were kids.

In school, Bonnie was the star pupil in her class. She was always winning prizes for writing essays, spelling, "speaking pieces," and things like that. Once, during her high school days, I remember that Cement City and Bryan High were in the spelling finals, and Bonnie, no bigger than a minute and looking like a fluffy-headed doll, spelled the entire class down and walked off with the medal for the city championship.

She had a lot of "fellers" in grade school — boys who thought she was too cute for anything. Bonnie always had a book satchel full of candy bars, chewing gum and sort of mashed looking apples that some little boy had brought her. But her pick of the lot was a boy named Noel. One day when she was about ten, he crossed her about something, and Bonnie followed him from school, caught up with him in front of the drug store and jumped on him with both hands and feet. When a passing neighbor woman separated them, Bonnie had a piece of razor blade in her hand threatening to cut Noel's throat for him if he ever made her mad again, and he was fairly blubbering, he was so scared.

I remember two sisters in Bonnie's class, who were notorious for stealing pencils. Aunt Em naturally didn't have much money for such things, and she used to insist that one pencil every two weeks was enough. These two girls took Bonnie's pencils several times, and after she was spanked at home for not being able to keep them, she confided to me that she was going to beat those girls to a pulp the next time they took anything of hers.

It wasn't long till they were again guilty, so Bonnie and I lured them down to the gravel pit and gave them the beating of a lifetime. Next day they were laying for us with their big brother along, but we took them on, big brother and all, and sent them flying, yelling for help. The pencil stealing stopped.

However, this is just one side of Bonnie's nature. For all of her pugilistic tendencies and her evident desire to fight at the drop of a hat, she was the tenderest hearted little thing that I ever saw. All you needed to do to make Bonnie cry was to start a sob story and begin bawling yourself. In five minutes Bonnie would be weeping copiously and ready to give you anything on earth she had if she thought it would help you out.

Her one overpowering devotion was for Aunt Em. We used to tease her about it and get her so mad she'd come at us with whatever she could find, even after she was grown.

When Aunt Em would go to work she threw her clothes just everywhere as she dressed. Billie wouldn't pick them up, but Bonnie would. She'd go around and gather up Aunt Em's slippers, pat them lovingly and set them in the closet; then she'd take Aunt Em's house dress and hang it up, caressing it like Aunt Em was inside of it. And all the time she'd be murmuring little things to the clothes, just like the baby talk she talked to her mother now and then, even after she was a great big girl.

One of the great jokes of Bonnie's rather pathetic little lifetime was that when she was seven, candidates in Cement City used to take her out with them to help them makes speeches before election time. Bonnie was so cute and so witty, and such a pretty little trick, that the candidates knew they could always count on getting crowds if they took her along. Considering that some of these same men she helped get elected later were pledged to hunt her down, this does seem like a gigantic and ludicrous travesty on life.

Although Bonnie had a lot of childhood sweethearts, she never had a date with a boy till she was fifteen. Soon after she began dating, she fell in love with Roy Thornton, a boy who was in school in Cement City. By the time she was sixteen, she and Roy were married.

When Bonnie loved, she loved with all her heart, and that was the way she loved Roy. When she was through with him, she was through. Bonnie was like that. She was loyal, too, even after she ceased to love Roy. That was why she never divorced him.

About the time Bonnie was married, I moved away with my husband to another town, and I wasn't with her again till after she met and fell in love with Clyde Barrow.

Mrs. Parker Goes On

Naturally, I didn't want Bonnie getting married when she was only sixteen, but she and Roy seemed so much in love and so determined that I gave my consent. They set up housekeeping just two blocks from me, but Bonnie just couldn't seem to stand being away from me. Every night of the world Roy had to bring her by to see me, and she was always begging me to go home and spend the night with them. It really became a joke with us, and we felt rather sorry for Roy, who was having a lot of difficulty with his honeymoon.

I remember one night it snowed and was terribly cold. Bonnie wasn't well and Roy wouldn't take her out in the snow to our house. About midnight she awakened him by crying, and said that she had just dreamed that I was dying. We had no telephone, and nothing would do Bonnie but that Roy must dress and go out in that blizzard to see if I was all right. Another evening, Roy came by the house and found me sick in bed. He wanted me to go home with him and spend the night. I said that I couldn't; I felt too wretched to walk the two blocks.

"Well," Roy said, gathering up a blanket, "I'll just wrap you up and carry you down there, mama, because I might as well not go home as to go without you. Bonnie would not let me in."

Finally I dressed and went. After a month of this sort of

goings-on, I told Bonnie: "Listen, if you're going to keep on being such a baby about your mama, you and Roy had better move in with me, because it'll be easier on all of us."

That suited them exactly, especially Roy, who was getting a little worn out, I'm sure, chasing down a mother-in-law every evening for his bride. They moved in. This was 1926 and Bonnie never left me again till she went away with Clyde Barrow in the spring of 1932.

We rented a house in Dallas about this time, over on Olive Street. After a few months, Roy began neglecting Bonnie, going off and staying days at a time. Bonnie went to the city and found a job at Marco's Cafe close to the court house on Main Street. Bonnie waited on tables at Marco's and helped at the cash register. Here, ironically enough, she met and became friends with the many officials and officers of the city, county, and state, who were destined by fate to spend two years tracking her to death.

The manager at Marco's was fond of Bonnie. He said she made friends easily and drew trade. He also complained to me that every bum down at that end of town had found out that Bonnie's heart was as big as the court house, and were working the life out of her for free meals.

"Mrs. Parker," he said, "it's got so Bonnie never draws a full pay day. She feeds everybody that comes in here looking hungry. The word is out and all those court house bums lunch off her all the time."

"She says it makes her miserable to think of anybody being hungry," I explained.

"Well, it's a dirty shame the way they impose on her," he

went on. "And if she doesn't stop it, I'm going to can her."

I talked to Bonnie about it and she promised to do better, but she didn't. Money never did mean anything to her. She'd either give it to me or to somebody with a hard luck story. She actually wouldn't buy herself enough clothes, and I'd have to go down and do her shopping when she became ragged. As long as she worked at Marco's, she fed people, and she never got fired for it, either. The cafe finally went out of business and Bonnie naturally lost her job. That was in November, 1929.

All newspaper and magazine stories concerning Bonnie's affair with Clyde, state that she met him while she was a waitress at Marco's Cafe, which is not true. Bonnie wasn't even working at Marco's when she met Clyde Barrow for the cafe was closed. She was visiting with a girl friend in West Dallas when she met Clyde, and the date was early in January of 1930.

By the second year of Bonnie's married life, Roy and she had been separated three times. I mean by "separated" that Roy would just walk off and leave her for a month or so, and then come strolling back some afternoon, expecting a big welcome, which he invariably got. All in all, I think they were separated like this about five times during the four years they were married. Bonnie used to get terribly blue when Roy would leave. She was crazy about him, though she never worshipped him as she did Clyde later. She certainly wouldn't leave her mother for him, which she did for Clyde, but she was still quite a kid about a lot of things. You see, she'd married when she was sixteen, and when this diary from which I'm going to quote, was written, Bonnie had been seventeen just three months. No seventeen year old girl was ever very profound. I'm quoting from the diary to show the simplicity of the life she led, and to refute the stories that at this time — or at any time — Bonnie was notorious in Dallas' night life, and the biggest "hotcha" girl in town. Bonnie was sitting home nights crying for her first love, and confiding her seventeen-year-old-sorrows to a dog-eared copy book.

The first entry is dated January 1, 1928, and starts off with this naive statement:

Dear Diary:

Before opening this year's diary, I wish to tell you that I have a roaming husband with a roaming mind. We are separated again for the third and last time. The first time, August 9-19, 1927; the second time, October 1-19, 1927; and the third time, December 5, 1927. I love him very much and miss him terribly. But I intend doing my duty. I am not going to take him back. I am running around with Rosa Mary Judy and she is somewhat a consulation to me. We have resolved this New Year's to take no men or nothing seriously. Let all men go to hell! But we are not going to sit back and let the world sweep by us.

January 1, 1928. New Years nite. 12:00.

The bells are ringing, the old year has gone, and my heart has gone with it. I have been the happiest and most miserable woman this last year. I wish the old year would have taken my "past" with it. I mean all my memories, but I can't forget Roy. I am very blue tonight. No word from him. I feel he has gone for good.

This is New Year's Day, Jan. 1. I went to a show. Saw Ken Maynard in *The Overland Stage*. Am very blue. Well, I must confess this New Year's nite I got drunk. Trying to forget. Drowing my sorrows in bottled hell!*

Bonnie seems to overlook the fact that her first entry is at midnight the night before and she was at home, safe and sound, with no "bottled hell" •round and nobody to drink it with, if there had been.

Jan. 2, 1928.

Met Rosa Mary today and we went to a show. Saw Ronald Coleman and Vilma Banky in *A Night Of Love*. Sure was a good show. Saw Scottie and gave him the air. He's a pain in the neck to me. Came home at 5:30. Went to bed at 10:30. Sure am lonesome.

Jan. 3, 1928

Searched this damn town over for a job today. I guess luck is against me. Haven't heard a word from Roy. I wonder where he can be. Diary, every night I look at his dear little pictures. That's all I have of him. I don't supose he wants me to know where he is. He doesn't love me any more. "Where is my wandering boy tonight?" I am fully discouraged, for I know I can never live with him again. I hunted up Reba Griffin today, just to know that she is not with him. She has taken my place in his heart but she will never take my place by his side. I am going to bed as it is 10:30. I wonder what tomorrow will bring.

January 4, 1928. Wednesday.

Stayed home all day and slept. Went to the Pantages tonight with L. T. Haven't heard from Roy yet. Lewis called me.

January 5, 1928.

Got a telegram from Harlingen. Little Roy is dead. Oh, wont our luck ever change? It is sure a lonesome old place tonight. I went with Lewis and Fred but I can't have a good time. I love my husband. I always think of him,. If God would only let me find where he is.

January 6, 1928.

Well, there's nothing to do all day. Just sit around. I went with Lewis tonight. Had a nice time, but I can't get Roy off my mind. We went out to Mae's awhile and went driving. Sure am blue tonite.

January 7, 1928.

Well, I went down town today and saw a picture. Milton Sills in "Framed." Sure was a good picture. Rosa Mary has been ill but is o. k. now. Tonight I went with Lewis again. Not a darn thing to do. I met Johnnie Baker tonite for the first time in a long time. Still the same old Johnnie. But I don't care anything about him.

Roy is always in my mind. I come home early tonite. I didn't feel like going anywhere much. Johnnie came out with Lew. Oh, God, how I wish I could see Roy! But I try my best to brush all thought of him aside and have a good time. If I knew for sure he didn't care for me, I'd cut my throat and say here goes nothing. Maybe he does though. I still have hopes. Raymond called me.* I have a date with him for tomorrow. But to hell with all men. He is very nice — a perfect gentleman. But how can I enjoy life? Raymond is a decetive (she means detective). I think I'll have him look Roy up. Gracie wants me to come down there but I can't bear to look at his sisters. They remind me of him. I love them because they are his. I took the blues when I went to see Mae. Well, maybe tomorrow will make things a little clearer.

*Not Raymond Hamilton. She did not know him until she met Clyde.

Jan. 8, 1928. Sunday.

It's just another day to me. Plenty to do but no heart to do it. Got up at 11. Raymond called and wanted a date with me, but shucks, I don't feel like going. I went to the Old Mill tonight. Was a very good show but I was bored to death. Had dinner after the show. Got home at 11:30. Lewis called me three times.

Jan. 9, 1928. Monday.

We have been torn up all day. Went to hunt a job but never found it. Got a letter from Gracie, but haven't heard from Roy. I guess I am a fool to look for any word from him but I don't want to lose hopes any worse.

Jan. 19, 1928. Tuesday.

Blue as usual. Not a darn thing to do. Don't know a darn thing.

Jan. 11, 1928. Wednesday.

Haven't been anywhere this week. Why don't some thing happen?

Jan. 12, 1928. Thursday.

Went to a show. Saw Florence Vidor and Clive Brook in "*Afraid to Love.*" Sure was good. Blue as hell tonight. Went to hunt a job at 903 South Harwood.

Jan. 13, 1928. Friday.

Went to a show. Saw Virginia Vallie in "Marriage."

Not a thing helps out though. Sure am blue. Everything has gone wrong today. Why don't something happen?

What a life!

Jan. 14, 1928. Saturday.

Went to town, saw a show, Wallace McDonald and Clara Bow in "*The Primrose Path.*" It was good. Not doing anything tonite.

Sunday, Jan. 15, 1928.

Went to grannie's today. Stayed home tonight. Nothing particular happened.

Monday, Jan. 16, 1928.

Went to Chocolate Shop today. Got a letter from Gracie. Sure am blue tonight. Have been crying. I wish I could see Roy.

Tuesday, Jan. 17, 1928 —

Thus ends the diary, with a date and a dash, and a plaintive wail for Roy, who was not to return to her till the following year. I hadn't interfered with Bonnie's affairs up till now, but she was so blue and so down, that it got under my skin. "Why don't you send him packing when he does come back?" I demanded of her, after finding her in tears one afternoon.

"Because I love him," she said.

"He treats you like a dish rag," I told her. "Comes and goes when he pleases. I'd put a stop to it if I were you, Bonnie."

She came and hugged me. "Someday I may get enough of the way he's acting," she said. "But right now I want him back, mama."

Well, what could a mother do? A girl in love has no sense anyway. About this time she began the job at Marco's Cafe, which she held till November, 1929. Work gave her something else to do besides brood, and she was soon in a better frame of mind. Her ruling passion all her life was babies. Clyde told me a month or so before he and Bonnie were killed, that she was always wanting to just "borrow" some woman's baby for a few days, and that he had his hands full with her sometimes when she'd get lonesome and blue for home. She'd sight a baby in some little town and begin to beg for the privilege of borrowing it till she got over the blues. "Hold-ups were things Bonnie never did get to really care for," Clyde said. "But the kidnapping racket was one where she'd have thrived, if all the people snatched had been one year old, or younger." I remember coming home from work one day while we were still living on Olive Street, and finding the house jam full of babies — black, chocolate, brown, even Mexican babies — for every sort and color of family lived around us. Bonnie and Billie were in the midst of all this gang of young ones, their faces beaming with happiness. "We've had a party," Billie cried. "And asked all the children in the neighborhood," Bonnie said, delightedly.

I could well believe them. I'd never seen so many babies before. "Listen here," I said, stepping over two youngsters covered with chocolate ice cream, "I can't get in the house. You've got to get these kids back to their homes right now."

Well, Bonnie and Billie delivered babies for the next two hours, and I never saw such a mess as that house was in, not to mention the invited guests. One negro baby was violently ill all night from having been fed too much chocolate candy by Bonnie, who was more generous than she was wise. One little one, too small to talk, was mislaid for awhile before the two girls finally located his mother and delivered him to her arms again, rather damp and sticky, but happy.

In the back of our yard a negro woman lived who had two pickaninnies who were very fond of Bonnie, and they used to climb up the magnolia tree in the alley and gather flowers for her every evening in the spring. They'd meet Bonnie when she came from work and present their bouquets, knowing that Bonnie would give them nickles, no matter if she had to walk to work next morning.

Early in 1929 Roy came back, but during the long separation, Bonnie's affection for him had cooled. She was going on nineteen now, and she was growing up. No longer was she the seventeen-year-old, whose girl friend was "somewhat a consulation." Nor was she the naive innocent who had tried "drowing her sorrows in bottled hell!" She was becoming a young woman and she was seeing Roy through new eyes. The marriage didn't last long this time, and it was Bonnie who sent Roy packing when the end of their love came, not Roy who deserted Bonnie.

The three children were still at home with me. Billie had married, but she and Fred lived with us. Bonnie lived a very ordinary, simple life. As I look back over it now, I realize that to all appearances, she was just an average girl with an average young girl's existence — not too much sorrow and not too much fun. About what one usually designates as middle class, I expect. There was nothing to mark her as out of the ordinary, nor to warn me that she was destined for a terrible future and a grim and revolting death.

Several months after the final break, her husband got into some trouble at Red Oak; was tried for robbery and sent up for five years. Bonnie was exceedingly sorry for him, but it didn't upset her as it once would have done, because she no longer loved him. She had beaus — she always had beaus — and went about to dances now and then, or to shows. But she made no effort to get a divorce, and when I asked her why, she said:

"Well, I didn't get it before Roy was sent up, and it looks sort of dirty to file for one now. Besides, I don't want to marry anybody else, so I'll just wait, mama."

She never got a divorce. She had no need of it then, and when she came to want one, she was a fugitive from justice and in no position to establish residence and file, because officers were looking for her and Clyde Barrow in every corner of the state. So she died Roy Thornton's wife in the eyes of the law, although she belonged wholly to Clyde from the instant she first laid eyes on him, for it was that sort of love.

I had never heard Clyde Barrow's name and didn't dream that such a boy existed till January, 1930. Bonnie, still out of work after the closing of Marco's Cafe, had gone to stay with a girl friend in West Dallas. This girl had broken her arm, and Bonnie went to help with the work. Clyde's folks lived near, and here it was Clyde came and met my daughter.

It all came about so simply, as such momentous and life-changing things often do. Clyde dropped by this girl's house, Bonnie was there, and they met. That was the beginning. I notice that newspapers and detective magazines state that the meeting occurred while Bonnie was working at Marco's Cafe; that Bonnie was seen often with Clyde in night clubs and speakeasies, Bonnie always smoking a big black cigar and paying all the bills. Sensation seekers abound, even among newspaper reporters, I see, and truth is never so interesting as a good, windblown yarn, made up out of whole cloth. Bonnie Parker met Clyde Barrow in the kitchen of a simple home in West Dallas, and at the time she met him, she did not know that he had ever had any trouble with the law.

If the simple recital of her diary doesn't prove to you that Bonnie wasn't the sort of girl who frequented night clubs and speakeasies, no denials I can make would convince you, anyway. As for the cigar smoking story, Bonnie never smoked one in her whole life, and it was the one newspaper story that made her the maddest, and which she begged me to refute. Reporters weren't interested in telling the world that Bonnie didn't smoke cigars. A cigar smoking gun moll made such lurid headlines, no paper would ever correct the story for me. Bonnie did smoke cigarettes, but not cigars. I was amused, though, to read one day where the law had discovered the Barrow gang's hide-out, and found several cigar butts with lip-stick on them. I wondered just which one of the boys had turned sissy on Clyde. The picture of Bonnie with the cigar was taken one Sunday afternoon in a moment of playfulness, just as young people the world over like to make pictures of themselves in some tough looking pose. In the Joplin, Missouri raid, the films fell into the hands of the officers, and the newspapers seized upon the finished product and printed them. From that day on, Bonnie was branded and nothing I could say would change it. It was one of the best stories which they used to make Bonnie seem tough, calloused, hard, coarse, and utterly beyond all human feeling.

I went over to see Bonnie and her friend about the second week in January, and here I saw Clyde Barrow for the first time. He was in the kitchen with a big cook apron on, mixing up some hot chocolate, a drink of which he was very fond. I knew there was something between them the minute Bonnie introduced him to me. I could tell it in Bonnie's eyes and her voice, and the way she kept touching his sleeve as she talked. I knew, too, that it was different from the young girl love she had given Roy. She was desperately afraid I wasn't going to like this Barrow boy, and she wanted me to like him above everything else. I sensed that.

A few weeks later Bonnie came home to stay, and that night Clyde called to see her. He intended leaving town next morning, and stayed late. So late, in fact, that I finally suggested that he'd better spend the rest of the night on the living room couch. I fixed him a bed and got him a pair of Buster's pajamas. He certainly was a likable boy, very handsome, with his dark wavy hair, dancing brown eyes, and a dimple that popped out now and then when he smiled. He looked more like a young law student or doctor than a bandit; he had what they call charm, I think. He was good company, and full of fun, always laughing and joking. I could see why Bonnie liked him.

It never entered my head that he was in trouble, or that he was leaving town because the town was getting too hot for him. If I had guessed that, I'd have sent him out of the house before daybreak. Not knowing any of these things, I helped Hubert and Fred off to work, and let Clyde sleep. He was still asleep when the officers came for him.

Clyde's older brother, Buck, had started his sentence at Huntsville in January, and when the officers awakened Clyde, one of them said to him tauntingly: "If you've got any rabbit in you, you'll run like Buck."

Clyde grinned at them and said sleepily: "Buddy, I'd sure run if I could."

When he was up and dressed, he went with them. I had my hands full with Bonnie while this was going on. I thought she was going crazy. She screamed and cried, beat her hands on the walls, begged the officers not to take him, hung around Clyde's neck — did all of the foolish, futile things a woman does under such circumstances. Clyde kept telling her it was going to be all right, but I could tell by the look on the officers' faces that they didn't think so. I asked them where they were taking him, and they said he was wanted in half a dozen places, but they were taking him to jail in Dallas first.

When they left, Bonnie stopped crying and just sat down like the end of the world had come. I had to go on to work, but I surely did hate to leave her there, so pathetic and help-less looking, with the tears rolling down her cheeks, crying silently. They kept Clyde in Dallas for several days and Bonnie went to see him whenever she could, and spent the rest of the time writing him volumes and crying silently. She couldn't talk about anybody else but Clyde. He seemed to be on her mind every minute. She'd ask over and over if there wasn't a chance that he might be freed of the charges. If he could just get out of this, she said, he'd never do anything else wrong — she knew it — she knew it! She began going out to see his mother a lot. It seemed to comfort her to be near anybody who was kin to Clyde. I didn't put any obstacle in her way, but let her do what she seemed to want to do. Of course, they wouldn't let her in to see him much, since she wasn't kin to him.

Her letters to Clyde Barrow during the time here and in Denton are, to me, the most pitiful and most revealing letters a woman ever wrote a man. And since they speak for themselves, I shall simply present them and let the reader draw his own conclusions as to whether or not Bonnie was already a tough and hardened woman of the world, ripe and ready for a criminal career.

1406 Cockrell Street, February 14, 1930.
Mr. Clyde Barrow,
Care The Bar Hotel,
Dallas, Texas.
Sugar:
   Just a line tonight. How is my baby by now? Today has been just another day to me and a hard one. Sure wish I could have seen you today. I think I could have made it. Maybe I can see you tomorrow. I went out to your mother's today. Marie is staying all night with me tonight.
   Honey, I don't know any news. Nothing ever happens any more. At least nothing interesting. I have had the blues

so bad all day that I could lie right down and die. I am so disgusted honey. I don't know what to do. I wish you were here to tell me what to do. Everything has turned out wrong. I even sprained my wrist today.

Sugar, when you do get out, I want you to go to work, and for God's sake, don't get into any more trouble. I am almost worried to death about this. Sugar, when you get clear and don't have to run, we can have some fun.

I sure hate to write when I feel as blue as I do tonight. I just called Nell and she said she saw you today. I sure do like her. She is so sweet. Darling, today is the first day I've cried in a long time but I sure did cry today all day. One of the boys brought me a box of candy for a Valentine today. I was alone with the baby (Billie, her sister's baby) and the idiot tried to spend the day. I never was so irritated in all my life. Talk about a sick woman but I was the sickest. I did everything but tell him to leave, and he stayed and stayed and stayed. Finally Billie came back and I walked out. Now, it's bad enough to be sick and discouraged as I was without having an idiot to put up with. I felt like throwing the candy in his face. I didn't appreciate the old candy at all, and I thought about my darling in that mean old jail, and started to bring the candy to you. Then I knew you wouldn't want the candy that that old fool brought to me.

Baby, how is Frank? (Frank Clause who was also in jail). He sure holds up well. He seems to be always smiling, and I guess he figures it's best to keep smiling. Darling, I hope you will always smile, because it kills me to see that awful look on your face when I start to leave you. It's bad enough to have to leave you, anyhow. Honey, I write books to you and only get little notes from you, but gee, how I love to get them. I wish I had a million because I have worn the ones I have completely out.

Honey, I sure wish I was with you tonight. I'm so lonesome for you, dearest. Don't you wish we could be together? Sugar, I never knew I really cared for you until you got in jail. And honey, if you get out o.k., please don't ever do anything to get locked up again. If you ever do, I'll get me a railroad ticket fifty miles long and let them tear off an inch every thousand miles, because I never did want to love you and I didn't even try. You just made me. Now, I don't know what to do.

And listen, honeyboy, you started this and somebody is sure going to finish it. Baby, — no, I didn't intend to call you that because you're not a baby. Well, darling, I'm going to have to close, as I can't seem to make this letter at all interesting. I have read it over and I can't seem to see any percentage in it at all. I'm so sorry, but I can't think of anything to say, only that I love you more than anything on earth, and I don't know if that is of any interest to you. When I find out for sure maybe I can write a sensible letter.

Tell Frank hello and not to be discouraged, because someday he'll be all right again. I hope you wont consider this letter preaching. Please pardon the mistakes, honey, but Marie has asked me ten jillion questions since I started writing. Tell Raymond (Hamilton) hell — no, I mean hello for me. I sure feel sorry for him. Just think: He has to spend two of the best years of his life in jail. Wouldn't that be awful, honey, if you had to? I'd just have to go down to the grave yard and wait. As it is, I can hardly wait. If you don't hurry and get out, I'm going to be hard to get along with. I would just simply die if you were convicted.

Honey, when I started to close this letter, Glynn said, "Don't stop. Write him a long letter, because he will have something to pass those lonely hours away." But I must stop, honey, as it is twelve o'clock, and Marie wont go to bed until I do. She's about to fall out now. Everyone says hello and they all wish you good luck. We think of you all the time. At least, you're on my mind all the time, and I keep the rest of them thinking about you by always talking about you.

Well, honey, I have to go to bed. I hate these long sleepless nights, but then time goes by as it always does, and maybe I can make it. Be sure to write me a long letter, honey, and think of me down here, thinking of you. I love you.

Just your baby,
Bonnie.

1406 Cockrell Street Wednesday night.
Mr. Clyde Barrow,
Care Denton County Jail,
Denton, Texas.
Dearest Little Darling:

Just a few lines tonight. How's my honeyboy? I guess you are surely lonsome. I didn't even know you'd gone till I borrowed the car and went down town and they told me you went away last night.* I was so blue and mad and discouraged, I just had to cry. I had maybelline on my eyes and it began to stream down my face and I had to stop on Lamar street. I laid my head down on the steering wheel and sure did boohoo. A couple of city policemen came up and wanted to know my trouble. I imagine I sure looked funny with maybelline streaming down my face.

Well, anyhow, I told them I merely felt bad and they offered to drive me home, but I thanked them and dried my eyes and went on out to your mother's. They weren't at home. I came back to town and couldn't find mother, so I went out to Bess's and couldn't find her. By that time I was on the verge of hanging myself, so I tried to wreck the darn car but didn't succeed, and came on home and walked the floor till now.

*Your mother and dad came out a few minutes ago. So
tomorrow I'm going to make an effort to see you. If I drive
all the way to Denton and still don't get to see you, it's going
to be "jam up" for somebody, because I'm sure going to be
hard to get along with. Darling, do you think of me? I never
was so unhappy in my whole life before. Dear, I don't know
what to do. I thought I would get a letter from you today,
but I don't suppose you have any stamps and paper, do you?*

*Sugar, I don't know a thing that is interesting, only I love
you more than my own life and I am almost crazy. Honey,
if you stay in jail two more weeks, I'll be as crazy as a
bughouse rat. I dreamed last night that you got "out" and I
got "in." I wish I could serve those long days for you, dear.
But if I were in, you'd probably forget me. This letter is like
all the rest. It is sort of melancholy, but sweetheart, I am so
moody, so discouraged and blue. You couldn't expect me to
be happy or even to write cheerful letters, for this is more a
strain on me, dear, than it is on you.*

*I promise you when you get out I will be happy and "never
cry 'no mo', 'no mo'." I wish I could cry on your manly
shoulder. If I even had some one who understands to tell me
what to do. I don't eat or sleep. You are driving me insane.
Dear, promise me you wont go away when you get out.
Honey, if you should leave me, I wouldn't know what to do.
Frank says you are going far away. I'm sure you wouldn't
leave me for him, would you? Of course, he says if you care
to have me go along, it'll be o.k. with him, but he says it in
rather a disinterested manner. I know you can't ever live in
Dallas, honey, because you can't live down the awful name
you've got here. But sugar, you could go somewhere else and
get you a job and work. I want you to be a man, honey, and
not a thug. I know you are good and I know you can make
good. I hope Frank will be a good boy when he gets out, for*

he is too young to start on that downward road.

Just think, honey, if you and he were to get twenty-five years in the pen! You would be a broken old man, friendless and tired of living when you did get out. Everyone would have forgotten you but me — and I never will — but I should more than likely be dead by then. And think, dear, all your best years spent in solitary confinement away from the outside world. Wouldn't that be terrible? Dear, I know you're going to be good and sweet when you get out. Aren't you, honey? They only think you are mean. I know you are not, and I'm going to be the very one to show you that this outside world is a swell place, and we are young and should be happy like other boys and girls instead of being like we are. Sugar, please don't consider this advice as from one who is not capable of lending it, for you know I'm very interested and I've already had my day, and we're both going to be good now — both of us. Oh, I'm so lonesome for you tonight and I'm hoping I'll be with you in a few days. Dear, I'm going to close and try and get this all in one envelope. Forgive this awful writing, but just thank goodness that I still have sense enough to write a sentence. Answer real soon, dear, and think often of

Your lonesome Baby.

P. S. I am coming up tomorrow, even if they don't let me see you, you'll know I came and tried. I love you. Be real sweet, honey, and think of the girl who loves you best. Try not to worry, for I do enough of that for us both. Everyone is o.k. and mother says hello, and she is hoping you can come home soon. I love you, darling, with all my heart, and maybe it wont be long till we can be together again. Think of me, darling, and what a wonderful time we will have when you come home — how happy we will be. I love you, honey.

Bonnie.

N. B. Note the extreme delicacy and tact with which the letter is worded. I went down town and "they told me you went away last night'* instead of saying "I went to the jail and the officers told me they took you to the Denton jail last night."

14-06 Cockrell St.
February 23, '30.
Honey Boy: —
    Just a line today as I have made another unsuccessful attempt.
    Sugar I am so blue I could die. I haven't gotten a letter from you this week. Dear, I went to Ft. Worth today to get some money and when I got up there nobody was home. I have become so discouraged I wish I was dead. I got the car the other day and your mother and I were coming up so I didn't meet her on time and she went on the bus. I started and the muffler come off and the durn car sounded like a thresher. I was going to take a chance on getting arrested anyhow but I ran out of gasoline and had to walk about 2 miles, and Honey it was sure raining. I got so wet I was terrible looking so I came back home. But listen, dear, I'm coming to see you tomorrow even if I have to walk every step 'cause honey, I can't wait any longer. I know I can get the car and if the darn thing breaks down I'll start walking and talking 'cause I must see my daddy.
    I saw Mr. and Mrs. Barrow yesterday. They came over to tell me about you. I was supposed to go out there this A. M. but I coasted over to "Cowtown" and your Sis from Denison is out there today and I have never met her. So I didn't want to go on that account. But I'm going out there tonight.
    Darling do you still love your baby? Say, honey, I have written you a letter every night but, dear, I didn't think you would be there long enough to get them. Sugar, maybe you

*won't be there long enough to answer. I love to get those
sweet letters from you but I had lots rather you would
answer in person. Every night I go to bed with hopes that
tomorrow might be brighter but it's always just another day.
Maybe it won't be this way always. At least if I thought it
would I would go down to the grave yard and wait. For I've
already found out life's not worth living without you.*

   *I've got a Majestic Radiola and they nearly drive me
crazy with the music. I love music but it always makes
me melancholy — and all I've heard today is "Lonesome
Railroad Blues" and "I sing all my love songs to you." It
nearly drives me mad. Dear, I had lots rather hear you
sing than Gene Austin. He's wonderful but he doesn't mean
anything to me. I know you think I have forgotten you
because I haven't written you or come to see you since you
went away but honey, if I could you know I would go to jail
for you and more than gladly with you. I only wish I could
serve those long old lonesome days for you. It hurts me lots
more to have you in there than it would be to be in there
myself.*

   *Dear, someone told Bud I got my divorce on the 18th
and he come out begging me not to get married again. He
said Edith told him I was going to get married the 25th of
February. He had been drinking as usual. I got so irritated
I almost screamed. If he hadn't left when he did I know I
would have "passed out." I hate him. I told him, No I didn't
suppose I was going to get married; at least I hadn't had
any late propositions. He says he thinks I should consider
his feelings before I do anything "rash," but I reminded him
that he wasn't in the "racket" any more. He said "Now what
would you do if I should tell you I was gonna get married?"
and I told him I would like to congratulate the young idiot
he married for taking a "pest" off my hands. He didn't see*

how Bonnie could talk that way — Anyhow as bad as he feels he would like to meet the "Lucky Dog" that made me care.

Honey, I don't know any news as nothing ever happens around here. Glynn is fine; he says tell you hello. Mother was coming up to see you today and we almost knew we couldn't get in so we are hoping we can see you tomorrow. Pat sure wants you to come to work.

He needs you bad. Now I want you to go back and stay with Pat 'cause you must help your Mother. She is sick and she needs you and I need you and I want you to stay here and be sweet.

Well I'll be a dirty name here it is tomorrow — What a silly remark — what I mean is I didn't finish my letter yesterday for I went back over to Ft. Worth and now it's 5:30 in the morning. I guess my sugar is sleeping by now. I had to get up early this A. M. as usual. But I have to get ready to go to Denton early. It looks as if it will rain today but just let it rain. I'll go anyway.

I'm sure tired this morning after driving so much yesterday. Honey, I don't know any news and it's too early in the morning to learn any, for no one is up but me. I'll have to close, baby, and here's hoping they let me see you today — Be sweet and write to me. I love you.

Just your baby,
Bonnie.

Evidence in Denton seemed insufficient to hold Clyde, and he was sent to Waco on March 2, 1930, where he confessed to two burglaries and five motor car thefts. He was given two years in prison on one charge, the others, totaling fourteen years in all, being held in abeyance. Bonnie was determined to go immediately to Waco to be with Clyde, and after quite a bit of argument at home, I consented, but only because Mary, Bonnie's cousin, who was married, had moved to Waco a few weeks before. I told Bonnie to go and stay with Mary till Clyde was moved to Huntsville to begin his term. Bonnie was so nearly out of her head with worry and grief that we all felt sorry for her, and felt that letting her go to Waco wouldn't hurt anything.

Accordingly, Bonnie left with Clyde's mother that same day, and both of them went to Mary's house. Clyde's mother spent only a night and day there, and then came home, but Bonnie stayed till Clyde made his jail break on March 11, just three days after his brother Buck had walked out of Huntsville.

Bonnie saw Clyde every day in Waco and sometimes twice a day; in between times she wrote to him. A sample letter shows how crazy the girl was about Clyde, and how determined to stay near him at all costs:

Waco, Texas.
March 3, 1930.
Hello, Sugar:
Just a line tonight, as I'm so lonesome. Just think, honey, today is the first time I have seen you in two weeks, and just a very few minutes today. But it sure was sweet just to get to see you. Those laws are all so nice, sugar. They aren't like those Denton laws.*

Your mother is spending the night with me tonight. I wanted her to stay so she could see you again tomorrow. Dearest, I'm going to get me a job and stay up here;
I couldn't make it in Dallas anymore without you. Sugar,

*how I wish you were out of all this awful trouble. I don't see
how I can get along if you go away. You didn't act like you
were very glad to see me today. What's wrong? Don't you
love me any more? I know how you feel, honey. I guess you
are awfully worried.*

*Listen, dear, I wont write much today, because I'll see you
tomorrow, we hope, and for a long old time. And honey, just
remember I love you more than anything on earth, and be
real real sweet and think of me, down here thinking of you.*

Your lonesome baby,

Bonnie.

*P. S. Don't worry, darling, because I'm going to do
everything possible and if you do have to go down, I'll
be good while you're gone, and be waiting — waiting —
waiting — for you. I love you.*

*This is the first time that Bonnie uses any of the slang of gangdom
Prior to this letter, she called them officers or policemen.

Mary accompanied Bonnie on all her trips to the jail
to visit with Clyde, and the boy's personality, even under
these adverse circumstances, was felt by Mary. She had
never seen Clyde Barrow till she saw him in the Waco jail
with a two year sentence hanging over him, but she told
me later that the first day she met him there behind the
bars, she thought he was the most charming and likable
young fellow she'd ever met, and remember that Mary was
twenty-three years old, and happily married, so her viewpoint was likely to be more sane and much less biased than
Bonnie's, where Clyde was concerned.

The rest of this story — the story of Clyde's jail break — is
something which I, her own mother, never learned till two

months after Bonnie was killed in 1934. Mary came to Dallas for the funeral and later told me the entire yarn. She had been afraid to talk about it before because she was afraid of the law, and also afraid that if her husband learned of her part in it, he'd be furiously angry with her. Unknown to the officers till the day this story sees print, Bonnie Parker, who had never been mixed up with crime or criminals before in her whole life, staged Clyde Barrow's jail break for him with all the coolness and daring of an experienced hand, which shows what love will lead a woman to do. But I'll let Mary tell the story.

Mary Relates

One of the boys in jail with Clyde was named William Turner, and his home was in Waco. He had a gun concealed in his house out in East Waco, but he didn't dare ask his sister or mother to bring it to him, fearing they might get caught in the attempt and be implicated. He didn't hesitate to use Bonnie for the purpose, if she was game. With the man she loved behind the bars, Bonnie was game for anything.

Accordingly, Turner drew a map of his house, where the key was to be found, the place where the gun was hidden, the place where the ammunition would be. His mother and sister both worked in the daytime, and he assured Bonnie there would be no trouble about getting in. Bonnie was to get the weapon, but that was only half the job. She then had to get it to Clyde in the jail without arousing suspicion and without getting caught.

Naturally, all this which I have just related was unknown to me at that time. I hadn't the least idea what we were getting into when we started out to East Waco. I knew Bonnie was going after something for the Turner boy, possibly some article of clothing. She ran errands for Clyde and his friends all the time, anyhow. It wasn't till we got out there and I found that nobody was at home, that I began to be worried. After Bonnie had located the key and walked in the door, she coolly informed me that she was after a gun so Clyde could make a jail break!

I never was so scared in my whole life. My feet were like ice and my knees like water. I just knew policemen were all around the house, waiting to pounce on us when we came out. I begged Bonnie to leave, but she said, no sir, she wasn't budging till she found that gun. When I saw that she was determined, I started in to help her hunt, for it seemed the quickest way to get away from there.

The gun wasn't where the Turner boy had said it would be, after all. In the end, we turned that house topsy-turvy before we found it in the window seat, and the place was in such an unholy mess that there was a big story in the papers next day about it's being ransacked, but nothing was said about the missing gun because the Turners didn't know it was there.

By the time we got the gun and started back to Waco, I was simply shivering with fright. I felt that everybody we passed knew we had a gun and were going to stage a jail break. Bonnie wasn't scared, though. She put on two belts, one under her dress to hold her slip tight to her body, and another on top. She slipped that horrible gun between her breasts in the pocket the two belts made.

We drove back to the jail, and Bonnie asked to see Clyde. The jailer said Bonnie had already been up to see Clyde once that day, and if she went up again, she must not stay long. Bonnie, backing off all the time, so that he wouldn't touch her and feel the gun, promised him that if she could see Clyde for just a minute she wouldn't bother the jailer again for a long time — and believe me, she meant that. It surely was going to be goodbye if she got the gun to Clyde. The jailer let her go up, and I sat down there perspiring as if it were summer time.

Finally Bonnie came back downstairs. We left as quickly as we could, and neither of us had anything to say. We drove home and went inside the house, locked the doors, pulled down the shades, and just sat there. The hours seemed like a million years. Finally it got dark, and we fixed a little supper and ate it. Luckily, my husband was out of town, for I'd never have been able to keep him from knowing something was wrong. We were both frightened now. Scared they'd shoot Clyde down when he tried to make his get-away; scared Clyde might shoot the officers, and be electrocuted or sent up for life. We didn't sleep all night, and at daybreak, Bonnie asked me to get a paper. There it was — the whole story. Clyde Barrow, Emory Abernathy, and William Turner had walked out of the jail to parts unknown. Nothing was said about where they got the gun.

Bonnie had a big cry after she read it. Then she straightened her face, and said: "Let's eat, Mary." After breakfast, Bonnie said, "I'll go to Dallas on the late interurban, Mary." We lay down on the bed, but though neither of us had closed our eyes all the night before, sleep wouldn't come now. Bonnie talked and talked — always about Clyde. He wasn't a bad boy, she said; he just hadn't a chance. If he got out of this mess and safely away, she'd get a divorce, go to him, and marry him. They would settle in some far off place and everything would be all right. Clyde wasn't ever going to do anything to get into trouble again. He had promised her and she knew he meant it, because he loved her. Over and over again — she couldn't talk about anything else.

Finally, we fixed something else to eat, and lay down again. It was dark now, but we had no lights on. We kept saying we must get some sleep, but we never did. Along about 9:30, we heard somebody outside and looked out the window. Two men were walking up the sidewalk. Bonnie began to tremble and I was on the verge of hysterics. They started pounding on the door. We lay there and listened and shivered. They pounded and pounded. They went across the street and sat on the curb and watched the house. After half an hour of this, they came back and pounded some more. It was nearly midnight before they finally went away.

Bonnie was afraid to take the interurban, bus, or train after that. She knew officers would be watching the stations to arrest her. At four o'clock in the morning I drove her out on the highway and put her out. She was going to "thumb it" into Dallas. She certainly was a forlorn looking little thing, starting off down that road alone in the cold gray dawn. I felt sorry for her, but I felt sorry for myself, too. I went back home and to bed, a nervous wreck.

Next day about noon two boys drove up to the house in a truck and asked for Bonnie. I said she'd gone to Dallas. "Well," one of them explained, "if you all hadn't stayed out all night last night, she could have had a ride with us. Her mother told us she was here, so we came by last night to get her, and boy, did we sit on that curb till it felt like the Rock of Gibraltar! What sort of a party did you two go on, anyway?"

I never did explain to them just the sort of party Bonnie and I had been on. I had an idea, that while the subject matter might be interesting, Bonnie and I would both be better off if I just let the idea ride that we'd spent the night out.

Mrs. Parker Continues

When Mary related this story to me two and a half years later, I clearly understood the significant part it had played in the shaping of Bonnie's future life in regard to law and order. Had I known about her part in the jail break, I should have undoubtedly conducted myself differently on several occasions, and used the most drastic methods possible to separate them before it was too late, even if it meant estranging Bonnie from me. I would have sent her away; I would have done anything, rather than permit her to continue in a path which could have but one ending — death and dishonor.

I'm sure this jail break and her own rather romantic and daring part in it made a lasting impression on Bonnie. In the first place, it had been accomplished so easily that she had never been suspected; in the second place, I'm sure that Clyde was very proud of her for being so plucky and courageous in circumventing justice and helping him get out of jail. He sent her a wire as soon as he got well away. The telegram came from Nokomis, Ill., and said that all was well. It also asked her to tell his mother, and sent her his love and a promise to write. I'm sure that he praised her highly for her courage and pluck.

Bonnie was a dramatist, born so. She loved being the center of things, and above everything else, she wished to please Clyde. I'm sure that she was flattered to think that she had measured up to his standards with a daring and grit which even the famous bandit, Belle Starr, couldn't have surpassed. But as I have said, a girl has two sides, one for the other fellow and one for her mother. I knew none of these things, just as I had known none of Clyde's mix-ups with the law till the officers came to arrest him at my house.

When Bonnie came home, she had nothing to say about Clyde's jail break, though she was very nervous. She grabbed the papers the instant they hit the porch, and on one or two occasions, went downtown to catch the early editions. The fugitives' freedom was short lived. They were captured March 18th in Middleton, Ohio, after they had robbed a dry cleaning establishment and the offices of the Baltimore and Ohio Railroad. They refused to divulge their true names, but the finger print system solved the mystery. The three were returned to Waco in a few days, and Clyde's entire sentence of fourteen years was invoked against him. He was to go to "The Walls," as they called Huntsville, at almost any instant, but for some reason, he was not taken till April 21, 1930.

I have none of Bonnie's letters to Clyde during the next two years, but I do have several of Clyde's to her. The first was in April on the 19th, two days before he left for Huntsville. Evidently they had had a spat over something, as the letter indicates. Clyde's letters were often badly misspelled, but his sentiments were still good and honest where Bonnie was concerned, at least, and his writings seem to indicate that he was contemplating doing the right thing when he got out of prison.

April 19, 1930.

Waco, Texas.

Dear Baby:

I just read your sweet letter, and I sure was glad to get it for I am awfully lonesome and blue. Why did you say you didn't know whether I would accept it or not?

Now, honey, you know darn well I didn't mean what I said in my last letter. I'm just jealous of you and can't help it. And why shouldn't I be? If I was as sweet to you as you are to me, you would be jealous too.

Say, sugar, these loco guys are making so much noise I can't write, so I will finish this tomorrow.

After a long lonesome night, I will try and finish. It's Easter Sunday and I sure wish I was outside with you. Gosh, honey, I bet we could have a good time today. Where were you last Easter, honey, and who was with you? Last Easter Frank Clause and I were together, as near as I can remember. Mrs. Vaughn sent me an Easter card yesterday but it wasn't near as pretty as the one you sent me last week.

Well, dear, I sure hope you don't have to work on Sunday. Well, you ask me if I wanted Bob to come up. You got my last letter, didn't you? That is all I am depending on now. I don't think I can get my time cut any. If Bob hasn't already left, send him as soon as you get this. I think maybe he can do me some good.

Sugar, I don't see why I didn't leave you a car so you could come down to see me on Sunday. This is such a pretty day and it is sure going to be a long lonesome one for me.

Well, baby, how are you liking your job by now? And have any of those hop-heads got smart with you? If they do, just remember the name, because I wont be in this joint all my life.

Just a minute, honey, and let me see what has happened up here. It's all right, baby, everything is o.k. I thought for awhile all of them were dead, for it was so quiet, but Frank is reading, and Pat is sick; two of them are asleep and Lee is sitting by the window looking out and wishing he was outside. This is the first time this place has been quiet since I've been here and I'm hoping they wont wake up till I get through writing.

Honey, you said you would do anything I wanted you to do. Well, I'll tell you what I want you to do. Just be a good little girl and always love me. If you'll do those two things, that is all that is necessary, except coming to see me and that is the main thing right now.

Say, Sugar, you ought to see me. I've got on Frank's suspenders, and I'm sure a darb of the season, no fooling. Honey, if I could just spend one week with you, I'd be ready to die, for I love you and I don't see how I can live without you. Say, honey, when I get down yonder and get to thinking of you, I'll jump right up and start towards Big D. I may not get very far, but I'll sure get caught trying.

Well, old dear, here's Bud Russell. I don't know whether he's going to take us up or not, but I guess he will. If he does, be sure and come down as soon as you *can. Honey, I don't know whether they're going to take me or not, but if they do, do what I told you. Come when you can . . .*

No, honey, they aren't going to take me this time and I am sure glad, for maybe I can get a chance to get my time cut again. Honey, Uncle Bud may come back tomorrow, but if he doesn't, I'll write to you. And if he does, I'll write to you as soon as I get to the Walls.

But I hope he doesn't come back for awhile.

Well, old sugar, I don't know any news, so I guess I will close. Send Bob as soon as you can. I love you.

Clyde.

P. S. When mama comes back up here, if she comes before I go down, tell her to bring me some old kind of shirt, so I can send this one home. It's too good to throw away. I love you.

Two days later Uncle Bud came back, and Clyde went down to The Walls for his stay of fourteen years. At first Bonnie was inconsolable. She cried constantly, and wrote long letters to Clyde every night. She had to work, and one can't wear grief like a garment and hold a job. Besides, she was a thoroughly normal girl, and in a few months began to take a new lease on life, and a new interest in the people about her. I don't know just when she stopped writing to Clyde, but I imagine it was along in the summer of 1930. Neither do I know just why she again took up the correspondence. I have two letters written in December of that year, from Clyde to her which indicate clearly that the correspondence had been broken off for some time, and that

Bonnie herself started writing again. In these two letters, quoted below, Clyde addresses Bonnie as his wife. This was necessary, according to prison rules, if he was to receive her letters. The men were allowed to write only to members of their families.

> *December 11, 1930.*
> *Dearest little wife:*
> *Just received your sweet and welcome letter, and believe me, it really gave me a great surprise to hear from you. Why honey, I couldn't hardly believe my eyes when I glanced at your handwriting on the envelope.*
> *So I took it and looked it over carefully and finally decided it was from you.*
> *Listen, Bonnie, who the h--- told you all those lies on me? Sugar, you know I didn't say anything like that about my little blue-eyed girl. Honey, I love you more than I love my own self and just because I have fourteen years is no sign I will be here always. Mother went to Waco to talk to the judge, and he said he would help her get my sentence cut back to two years. If everything works out like I hope it will, I wont have to stay away from my baby much longer.*
> *Say, honey, I know your mother thinks I didn't want to answer her letter, but you see, Sugar, I am not at the same camp I was when she wrote me, and at this camp you can't write to anyone except your family. Be sure and tell her how it is. I am on Eastham Farm No. 2 and I get my mail at the same address, Weldon, Texas, Box*

16, Camp No. 2, so be sure and answer this as soon as ever you get it, for honey, I sure do need your letters to pass away these long lonesome days.

I would give anything on earth if I could get one more good look at my little blue-eyed baby. Honey, I haven't even got a picture of you, for when I left Camp No. 1 it was unexpected, and I didn't have time to get your picture, so please send me another if you have any.

Well, baby, I am going to close for this time, and if you answer this, I will write more next time. I send all my love to you from your daddy that loves you.

Clyde Barrow.

December 21, 1930.

To my darling little wife:

Hello, honey. I received your most sweet and welcome letter last night and honey, you'll never know how glad I was to get it, for now I can enjoy Christmas. Sugar, what made you think I wouldn't answer your letters? Why, darling, you know I love you more than anything, and you haven't done anything to me. Listen, Sugar, mother is not mad at you. She was down here last week and she asked me about you. Said she would like to see you, and I told her she didn't want to see you half as much as I did, which is really true for I am just crazy to see my little blue-eyed girl.

You asked me if I heard from Frank or Gladys. No, dear, I haven't and I don't care to, for they don't care anything about me and I am not mad about them. All

I ever want for is you, Sugar, and I would give my right eye to see you. And if you can come I want you to come and see me. I can get L.C. to bring you, for I know you haven't the money to come down here with. But it wont be like that always darling. Some day I will be out there with you and then we can be happy again.

Sugar, mother just about got my time cut to two years, and I have been down here eight months already.

If she does get it cut, it wont take long for me to shake it off. So you just make it the best you can till I do, and then let me do the rest.

Well, old dear, I don't know any news as usual, so be a sweet little girl and write your daddy real often, because I really enjoy your sweet little letters. Tell everyone hello for me, and I wish you a merry, merry Christmas. Answer real soon. I send all my love to you.

Your loving husband,

Clyde Barrow.

P. S. Please send me one of your pictures.

Bonnie didn't talk to us about Clyde as much as she had at first, and a few months later she began going with a young man whom I shall call Tom. I was more relieved than I would have admitted to anyone, and thought that Tom was the answer to Bonnie's problem, after all.

When Clyde came home from jail the next year, I found out I'd been mistaken.

Nell Goes On With the Story

My mother never ceased in her efforts to get Clyde's sentence cut from fourteen to two years. For many months it looked as if she would not be successful. Things had become complicated for Clyde before this was accomplished. Clyde himself had no knowledge that the sentence was to be cut until just a few days beforehand, and he was very discouraged and blue.

Of course, prison life is no picnic. It isn't supposed to be. Clyde was just twenty-one when he went to jail, and despite his criminal tendencies to steal, and his disregard for law and order, he was still the sweet and likable brother I had grown up with. But prison life did things to him which changed that.

I've no intention of writing an expose of the prison systems of America. In fact, after seeing "*I Am A Fugitive From A Georgia Chain Gang,*" I am confident that Texas prison systems are paradises compared with what is alleged to take place in some states. Clyde was treated badly in many instances, according to things he told us, and occurrences in the Walls and at the farms were terrific factors in shaping his future life.

For one thing, he saw a "lifer" knife a young boy to death before his eyes one night. The man knew he was immune from a death sentence and he had nothing to lose. He had a row with the boy and killed him brutally. The "lifer" was given solitary confinement and changed to another place, but nothing else was done to him. The incident ate into Clyde's mind.

Once I visited him and found him with both eyes blackened. Since the guard was ever present on these visits, I had no chance to get the details till later, but I then learned that Clyde had received a beating because he had complained in the field that the pace set for chopping cotton was too fast for him. He also told us that often the guards would ride them down if they lagged behind in their work. Once, after I had been with him, he said the guard accused him of having passed a note to me. Although Clyde denied it, the guard beat him severely for it. Of course, the guard could have saved trouble all around by having me searched before I left the prison, but this idea apparently didn't occur to him.

Clyde had worked in the fields till he came to Dallas in 1922. He was used to it, but he said the work there was too heavy for him. When the long days were finished the convicts were returned to the farms, and were forced to run all the way. The guards were behind them on horseback, and if they failed to keep the pace, they were slated for punishment. I never saw the men come in from the day's work and have no way of knowing how it was done. My sister-in-law, Blanche, once went down to visit Buck, and parked beside the fields waiting till the men went in. She told me that the prisoners ran the whole two miles, just as Clyde had said.

When you have a loved one in prison, your sympathies are going to be with him, and often the things you learn and suspect drive you nearly crazy. I tried not to think of what might be happening to Clyde during those two years, and spent my efforts in trying to have a job waiting for him when he did get out. I was determined that Clyde should be a man, as Bonnie had said, and not a thug.

Buck, we felt, was finally headed on the right path. He met and married a splendid, gentle, good country girl named Blanche Caldwell. A few weeks after he married her, he told her he was an escaped convict, and Blanche prevailed on him to come home and talk things over with his folks. She wanted a man for a husband; not one who must sneak and hide. Blanche wanted Buck to go back and serve his time, as did my mother. Accordingly, December 27, 1931, we gave the Huntsville officials the shock of a lifetime by driving up and knocking on the door and asking them to please let Buck come inside.

Naturally, this action on Buck's part, and his statement that he meant never to do anything to get in trouble again, was greatly in his favor. We felt that he too, would not have to serve his full time, and that both boys, with splendid girls waiting for them, would settle down and really do the right thing.

Just before Clyde was released, in a moment of despondency, despair, and utter hopelessness with life, he had asked a brother convict to chop off his two toes with an ax so that he would be taken within the Walls and released from drudgery in the fields. This revolting incident had just occurred when Clyde's pardon was obtained on Feb. 2, 1932. He came home to us on crutches.

My sister and I took him down town when he arrived, and bought him a complete outfit, except shirt and gloves. Clyde insisted on a silk shirt and kid gloves.

"Why, Clyde," I remonstrated, "you don't want an old silk shirt."

"But I do," Clyde insisted. "And I mean to have it." "Listen, honey," I tried to explain, "nobody but bootleggers and gangsters wear silk shirts. Nice people just don't go in for them, that's all."

"I'm going to have a silk shirt," Clyde said, and walked us all over town till we found one.

Back home that night, my sister and I had a serious talk. "I don't like it," I said. "There's a new air about him — a funny sort of something that I can't put my finger on — but Clyde's changed. I'm afraid he's not going to go straight, Sis. I don't like that silk shirt business at all. It isn't like the Clyde I used to know." Clyde came out of his bath about that time and began putting on his newly purchased finery. We both tried to talk to him. "Honey," I said, "what you ought to do now is to get you a job and a good girl and get married and settle down."

"I had a good girl before I went away," Clyde returned, tying his tie with a certain swagger. "I'm going to doll up now and go over there and see if Bonnie will still speak to me. Maybe not. No decent girl would, I suppose."

It turned out that Bonnie would.

Mrs. Parker Takes Up the Story

When Clyde walked up to the door that night, Bonnie was sitting in the living room with Tom. The instant she looked up and saw Clyde, it was just like he'd never been away at all. She jumped up and ran to him where he stood, looking at the two of them, sort of uncertain and defiant, and she went right into Clyde's arms.

"Oh, Clyde — darling!" was all she said before he kissed her, but it seemed to be enough. Tom got up and went home.

I was in the kitchen, and after a little while I called Clyde and asked him to come out and talk to me. "Listen, Clyde," I said, "if you want to go with Bonnie, that's all right with me. But I want you to get a job first and prove to me that everything is going to be all right."

He was looking boyish and engaging again, his dimple and smile working. Bonnie was hanging around his neck, perfectly radiant, like a fire had been turned on inside of her. The crutches didn't seem to be noticed by either of them. Clyde sat down in the kitchen chair, parked the crutches and pulled Bonnie over on his knee. "Shucks," he said, kissing Bonnie's cheek, "no decent girl would go with me, would they, honey?"

Bonnie just kissed him back and giggled.

"Now, don't talk that way, Clyde," I said. "Many a good boy has gotten in trouble and gone to the pen. There's no reason why you can't make good and go straight."

"Nobody would give me a job," he insisted. "Nell says she's got one for me — but it's way up in Massachusetts."

"Maybe you'd get to like it up there," I said. "And surely that's far off enough that the law wouldn't be knowing you every time you stuck your head out of the door. Things would work out. If you and Bonnie love each other, I'm not going to stand in your way at all."

He thanked me. He was always polite and courteous to me. He said he did mean to do everything he could to keep out of trouble, but that he didn't think he'd have much luck in Dallas, with smart cops running him in every time they saw him. I told him I didn't think it would be that bad. I went off and left him and Bonnie alone in the kitchen for awhile, because I knew that they had a lot to say to each other.

Clyde was around the house all the rest of February, and then Nell really got him the job. She got it through a friend of hers who was with a construction company in Wooster, Mass. Clyde was able to walk nicely by that time, and all of us felt very happy about the matter. I know Bonnie did, although she hated to have him go away.

But the job didn't last. By the end of the first week, Nell's friend had written that he was afraid Clyde wouldn't make a go of it. He said the boy seemed restless and nervous, and couldn't seem to settle down and get into the swing of the work. He was afraid it just wasn't going to turn out well.

He was right. At the end of two weeks Clyde was back home again. It was along about the 17th or 18th of March, as I recall, because on the 20th, Bonnie left home. Clyde's excuse for coming back was that he simply couldn't work. He said he was always looking over his shoulder, expecting to see an officer bearing down on him; that he lived in daily and hourly fear of arrest, and that the horror of prison was always with him. When Nell pointed out that if it was like that in Massachusetts, it would be worse in Texas, he said: "If I've got to hide and run away from the law all my life, I want to be around where I can slip back and see my folks, anyhow. Gosh, Sis, I nearly died of lonesomeness up there. I've been away from you all two years. I've got to stay close to home."

This passion for having to see his folks was one of the reasons that Clyde was finally caught, for he and Bonnie came home to see us often till the day they died.

Bonnie told me a few days after Clyde returned that she had a job with a cosmetic company demonstrating their face creams and lotions, and was going to Houston. She'd never left me before, but times were bad and jobs were hard to find. I never had any reason to believe that Bonnie would deceive me and I believed what she told me. She did have the job. I made sure of that, and let her go, never suspicioning a thing. Two days later I heard from her. She was in jail in Kaufman!

Only a mother can appreciate my feelings when I walked into that Kaufman jail and saw Bonnie behind the bars. Death would have been much easier. In fact, death was not even a tragedy when compared with the events I was to live through during the next two years. Bonnie cried a little when she saw me. The jailer and his wife, Mr. and Mrs. Adams, were very nice to her. They let her sit on the lawn in the evenings and romp with their children. She wasn't treated like a criminal at all, but this didn't change the fact that Bonnie was in jail. Nothing could change that.

We had several long talks and Bonnie told me everything. She had been with Clyde and another boy, who was also in jail. They had planned a robbery and were surprised before they had accomplished it. Running away in a stolen car over country roads, they stuck in the mud, and had to take to the fields. The officers were hot after them, and in desperation, they caught some mules in the field and tried to ride them in an attempt to get away. The mules exercised the immortal prerogative of mules and refused to budge. When it became plain that the mules weren't going anywhere, they abandoned them and again ran through the fields, the bullets whistling over their heads as they ran. Bonnie lost her slippers in the soft earth and Clyde had to carry her.

Finally she and Clyde tumbled into an irrigation ditch, and here they stood, clinging to each other. "Well," Clyde had said, "this looks like where we get ours, honey."

When the gunfire died down a little, Clyde, still carrying her, found a deserted country church and hid Bonnie in it. "I'll get a car and come and get you," he promised, and went away. Bonnie waited in the darkness, cobwebs around her, bats whizzing past, and somewhere a hoot owl cried dismally. Once the officers came by and debated whether or not to enter the church, then decided against it and went on. The hours grew, and Bonnie decided something had happened to Clyde. She left the church. Her idea, she said, was to get out on the highway, and if Clyde didn't come along, to hitch hike her way back to Dallas, but the officers caught her. They also caught the other boy, but Clyde escaped.

Bonnie and the other boy refused to tell the name of the other person with them. Bonnie was being held for questioning by the grand jury. I started to make bail, but Mrs. Adams stopped me. "Don't do it, Mrs. Parker," she said. "I know you haven't the money for bond, and she's not going to need it. They really haven't a thing against her, and when the grand jury meets in June, they'll give her a no-bill. Let her alone. She's not suffering, and time to think matters over may mean all the difference in the world to the child in the future."

That wasn't the reason I left her there. I didn't make bond for Bonnie because I really was in bad financial straits and couldn't very well spare the money. I came home and left her in jail in a cell next door to a crazy negro woman. All in all, it was enough to break a mother's heart, but I was to learn later that the human heart can stand many, many breakings and still keep right on beating.

Bonnie stayed in the Kaufman jail three months — something that Dallas officers don't know till this day. When she and Clyde were killed and their past histories were on every front page in America, reporters and policemen dug far back into records trying to find something on Bonnie and were never able to produce one bit of proof that she was ever in trouble with the law for anything till she became famous as Clyde's companion. The Kaufman thing was never mentioned. In fact, so clear was Bonnie's record that they didn't take her fingerprints till after she was dead. Why they did that, I'll never know. Finger prints are useful only when the criminal is alive, I thought, and Bonnie was beyond ever being alive again, but the law apparently required them for its files.

It was while Bonnie was in Kaufman waiting for the grand jury to meet, that she wrote her "Suicide Sal" poem. Bonnie was "Sal" and Clyde was the perfidious "Jack" who threw Sal down. That poem in Bonnie's own handwriting, written on leaves of a cheap notebook, is still in my possession and it is a revelation in psychology. Compared with her other letters written to Clyde, it shows a definite change in mental attitude, and an attempt at assimilation of underworld atmosphere which is far from healthy.

Before Bonnie went out on the road with Clyde Barrow as an outlaw, her letters had been perhaps a bit sticky with sentiment, but very lucid, very human, and very much the sort the average young girl writes when she's in love. Also, these letters repeatedly beg Clyde to keep out of jail and go straight.

It is clear from the numerous quotations used in the poem that Bonnie was learning the jargon of gangdom, and striving desperately to fit into it and become part of it. This bit of writing reminded me of a small child who learns certain grown-up words and says them over and over, often incorrectly and inappropriately, in order to prove to adults that he is getting on. I shall present the poem and ask those interested in the psychological side of this story to compare Bonnie's diary and letters written before she met Clyde with this attempt at poetry, written after she'd been associated with him the two months following his release from prison. I realize that I am not learned in such matters, but to my inner consciousness there seemed to be a strange and terrifying change taking place in the mind of my child.

THE STORY OF SUICIDE SAL

We each of us have a good "alibi"
For being down here in the "joint;"
But few of them really are justified
If you get right down to the point.
You've heard of a woman's glory
Being spent on a "downright cur,"
Still you can't always judge the story
As true, being told by her.
As long as I've stayed on this "island,"
And heard "confidence tales" from each "gal,"
Only one seemed interesting and truthful —
The story of "Suicide Sal."
Now "Sal" was a gal of rare beauty,
Though her features were coarse and tough;
She never once faltered from duty
To play on the "up and up."
"Sal" told me this tale on the evening
Before she was turned out "free,"
And I'll do my best to relate it
Just as she told it to me:

I was born on a ranch in Wyoming;
Not treated like Helen of Troy;
I was taught that "rods were rulers"
And "ranked" as a greasy cowboy.
Then I left my old home for the city
To play in its mad dizzy whirl,
Not knowing how little of pity
It holds for a country girl.
There I fell for "the line" of a "henchman,"
A "professional killer" from "Chi;"
I couldn't help loving him madly;
For him even now I would die.
One year we were desperately happy;
Our "ill gotten gains" we spent free;
I was taught the ways of the "underworld;"
Jack was just like a "god" to me.
I got on the "F. B. A." payroll
To get the "inside lay" of the "job;"
The bank was "turning big money! "
It looked like a "cinch" for the "mob."
Eighty grand without even a "rumble"—
Jack was last with the "loot" in the door,
When the "teller" dead-aimed a revolver
From where they forced him to lie on the floor.
I knew I had only a moment—
He would surely get Jack as he ran;
So I "staged" a "big fade out" beside him
And knocked the forty-five out of his hand.
They "rapped me down big" at the station,
And informed me that I'd get the blame
For the "dramatic stunt" pulled on the "teller"

Looked to them too much like a "game."
The "police" called it a "frame-up,"
Said it was an "inside job,"
But I steadily denied any knowledge
Or dealings with "underworld mobs."
The "gang" hired a couple of lawyers,
The best "fixers" in any man's town,
But it takes more than lawyers and money
When Uncle Sam starts "shaking you down."
I was charged as a "scion of gangland"
And tried for my wages of sin;
The "dirty dozen" found me guilty —
From five to fifty years in the pen.
I took the "rap" like good people,
And never one "squawk" did I make.
Jack "dropped himself" on the promise
That we make a "sensational break."
Well, to shorten a sad lengthy story,
Five years have gone over my head
Without even so much as a letter —
At first I thought he was dead.
But not long ago I discovered
From a gal in the joint named Lyle,
That Jack and his "moll" had "got over"
And were living in true "gangster style."
If he had returned to me sometime,
Though he hadn't a cent to give,
I'd forget all this hell that he's caused me,
And love him as long as I live.
But there's no chance of his ever coming,
For he and his moll have no fears

But that I will die in this prison,
Or "flatten" this fifty years.
Tomorrow I'll be on the "outside"
And I'll "drop myself" on it today:
I'll "bump 'em" if they give me the "hotsquat"
On this island out here in the bay . . .
The iron doors swung wide next morning
For a gruesome woman of waste,
Who at last had a chance to "fix it."
Murder showed in her cynical face.
Not long ago I read in the paper
That a gal on the East Side got "hot,"
And when the smoke finally retreated,
Two of gangdom were found "on the spot."
It related the colorful story
Of a "jilted gangster gal."
Two days later, a "sub-gun" ended
The story of "Suicide Sal."

Bonnie was lodged in the Kaufman jail on March 22, 1932. On March 25, Clyde staged a robbery in Dallas, Texas, and made good his escape. This was at the Sims Oil Co. The manager, down at headquarters, identified the bandit as Clyde Barrow by pictures. Since Bonnie was not at home nor working in Dallas, she was supposed to have been with him, and the order for Clyde's arrest was made to include her also. She was said to have waited outside for him in a car. Already, the legend of Bonnie Parker, the girl with the "bright yellow hair," was beginning to grow, and on every occasion that Clyde was implicated in anything, Bonnie was reported to have been with him, whether she was or not. Twice during her stay in the Kaufman jail, newspapers stated that Bonnie was with Clyde, when it was humanly impossible for her to have accompanied him. Once in August, when the killing at Atoka, Oklahoma, occurred, Bonnie was said by the papers to have been Clyde's companion. As a matter of fact, she spent the night with me, and Dallas officers knew it, because they checked up.

On April 27, Clyde was charged with his first murder — the Bucher killing at Hillsboro. Clyde insisted till the day he died that he had nothing to do with that murder, and since he later killed so many men and admitted the killings to us, I believe that he told us the truth about the Hillsboro affair. Again newspapers stated that a girl with bright yellow hair waited outside for him in the car, but Bonnie had another month or two in the Kaufman jail yet. As to the Hillsboro affair, I was not hearing from Clyde then, and Nell is far more competent to relate the story of what really happened, according to Clyde's version.

Nell Tells the Story

When Clyde left home with Bonnie, our family was as ignorant of what was going on as Mrs. Parker. We had no idea the two were together, though good common sense should have told us, I suppose, that they weren't likely to be separated. You must understand, if you can, that we never believed anything bad we heard about Clyde until he told us with his own lips. Newspaper stories sometimes frightened us, but we refused to believe them till we had confirmation. We realized that Clyde was restless, unhappy, and not at all like he had been before he went to prison, and we were willing to humour him and let him get his bearings again, if that was what he needed. We would have objected with our last breaths, to his taking to the road and living by what he could steal. We didn't know it till word came from Mrs. Parker that Bonnie was in Kaufman, and that Clyde had been with her.

Although he was implicated, we did not believe that Clyde had killed old Mr. Bucher in Hillsboro. The next day after the killing, I went out to my mother's to see if there had been any word from Clyde. He was hiding behind the house, mother said, and I went out to talk with him. I asked him if he had been mixed up in that Hillsboro thing and he said, "No, Sis, good God, no! I told those dumb eggs not to use any gun play — and I beat it the minute I heard the bullets popping."

"Oh," I cried, "so you were with them, then? I thought you said you weren't."

"Listen, Sis, don't start bawling me out," he begged. "I'm near enough crazy as it is. I was with them — I meant to take my share of the money — I'm not denying any of that. But you see, it was this way. When we walked into that store of Mr. Bucher's the first time to look the joint over, Mrs. Bucher was there, and she recognized me and I her. She used to live in Dallas and I went around with her boy some. So when we got out of the place, I said to the boys: 'I can't have anything to do with this, because that woman knows me as well as she knows her own son.'

"We fixed it up, then. I was to sit outside in the car and they were to go inside pretending to want to buy some guitar strings, offer a big bill as payment, and get old man Bucher to open the safe. Then they were going to hold him up and take the money. I told them two or three times to be careful about any gun play. I said, 'You start anything, and we'll be sunk, because Mrs. Bucher will remember me, and they'll catch us all.' Well, they promised. The two boys — one was almost twice as big as I am — went in according to arrangements, but they thought that Mr. Bucher would open the safe. It turned out that he called his wife to do it. I don't know how the shooting started — I just heard somebody scream, and guns popping, and I stepped on the gas and beat it. I don't know how they got away and I don't care."

Well, of course, Mrs. Bucher identified Clyde and also Raymond Hamilton later. I'm sure she identified Clyde because she knew he'd been with them on the first trip, but why she said Raymond was along I don't know. Clyde had never been with Raymond on any job at that time. He hadn't met him till 1930, and had not teamed up with him at this time. Clyde told me the names of the two boys who did the killing. They're both serving time now for burglary but were never implicated in the Hillsboro murder. It's still pinned on Clyde and Raymond. Not that it matters, considering how many terrible things Clyde and Raymond did eventually; I'm just trying to set things down as they really happened, and show how one thing led to another, each one getting Clyde in just a little deeper, till in his mind there wasn't a chance for him to do anything but go on as he did. Please understand that I realize fully that Clyde didn't have to steal in the first place; that the first offence needn't have been followed by a second; that when he came from prison, he could have stayed on the job in Wooster, if he'd put his mind to it; and that after he came home, he could have begged or starved rather than become an outlaw and a fugitive again. I realize fully all of these things and I'm not excusing Clyde. I'm just telling.

On May 5th, five days after the Hillsboro affair, two bandits robbed the Magnolia station at Lufkin, and kidnapped the manager. Four blocks down the street they repeated the performance at the Gulf station, and kidnapped that manager. The headlines screamed that Bonnie and Clyde were at it again, and both kidnapped men, when released, identified pictures in the rogue's gallery as Clyde and Frank Clause. Clyde told me later that he wasn't in on that, either, and certainly Bonnie wasn't, because she was still in the Kaufman jail. As I have said, we believed Clyde when he said he didn't do a certain robbery or murder, because he admitted so many crimes to us, often crimes that the law knew nothing about. Why should he lie to us? What was one robbery more or less during a spring and summer that was filled, not only with robberies, but murders?

At this time it became the fad to recognize Clyde Barrow as the principal in every crime committed in Texas, and always there was a girl with bright yellow hair in the car, waiting. She was not, however, smoking big black cigars, although the whole world now believes that Bonnie smoked them from the first, so potent is the power of suggestion. But the picture of Bonnie with the cigar wasn't discovered till April of 1933 in a tourist camp in Joplin, Missouri.

Yet, if you read the stories in the blood and thunder magazines, you will learn that Bonnie Parker was notorious in Dallas for years before she met Clyde as one who smoked cigars constantly in public. Don't get me wrong. I'm not trying to make an angel out of Bonnie. The truth is fair and right, even to a murderer, and legends and traditions have grown up around this girl, manufactured out of whole cloth without one word of truth to back them, which when looked at in the cold light of reason and factual evidence, simply cannot stand up.

Mrs. Parker Resumes

Meantime, in Kaufman, the grand jury met. They had Bonnie up before them, questioned her about many things, and as Mrs. Adams had predicted, they nobilled her on June 17, and she came home to me. She was soberer, more quiet, and a great deal older than the Bonnie who had left home three months before. It was evident that she had been doing a lot of thinking. We talked the situation over and I pointed out to her the trouble she had caused herself by following her heart instead of her head. "If Clyde's going to keep on the way he's been going," I said, "you're going to have to stay away from him."

She looked at me soberly. "I'm through with him," she told me. "I'm never going to have anything more to do with him." Then she went out of the room rather quickly and I suspected she'd gone to have a good cry.

She stayed in Dallas till the last of June, looking for work, and having very little to say. I felt sorry for her, but I felt too, that time would heal the wound and she'd find other interests and be able to forget Clyde. I didn't want her to go to him. What mother in her right mind would want such a thing to happen to her daughter? Clyde was a marked man, and no good could ever come of Bonnie's being with him, no matter how much they loved each other. One day in June, I came home from work and my mother told me that Bonnie had gone to Wichita Falls, where she had heard of an opening in a new cafe. It seemed queer that Bonnie would leave me without saying goodbye. Something whispered to me that she'd gone to Clyde, but I shut it in the back of my mind. I didn't want to believe that. Besides, in a few days I had a letter from Bonnie, telling all about the new job, where she was staying, and what hours she was working. I heaved a sigh of relief.

It was not till August that I saw Bonnie again. She came back to see me then. It was Friday, the fifth, I remember, because that was the night that it was reported that Clyde and Raymond Hamilton murdered two officers at Atoka, Oklahoma. Bonnie came by the place where I worked and wanted me to go home with her then. She said she'd be in Dallas only a day or two. I couldn't get off at that hour, so I sent her on home, and the forewoman let me leave at 4:30. Bonnie was at home with Billie and the baby when I reached there, and we had a grand reunion when all the family came in from work. I never was so glad to see a person in my life. She hadn't changed a bit that I could see, except that she seemed nervous, jumped at the slightest noise, and kept looking out of the windows constantly.

It was hot, and Bonnie said the hours in the cafe were pretty long, and she had been working hard and was pretty well worn out. I babied her a lot. Bonnie was so little and she could be so pathetic looking when she was tired or not feeling well. I didn't mention Clyde to her till late that night when we were sitting on the porch alone. I asked her then if she'd seen him and she denied it vigorously. "You know I wouldn't have anything to do with him, mama," she said.

"Not after the trouble I got into down in Kaufman. No, I haven't seen him and I don't want to see him." It didn't seem sensible that she would, and I believed her. You see, I wanted to believe her more than anything in the world. Besides, Bonnie had never lied to me before this. (I discovered later that she was lying to me about everything.)

For instance, Clyde himself had brought Bonnie to Dallas four days before, and she had spent the day at Clyde's home. They had arrived early on the morning of the first, coming from Wichita Falls, where Bonnie, Clyde, and Raymond had been living in a rented cottage ever since the last of June. Clyde and Raymond were planning to stick up the Neuhoff Packing Company that day. They had already gone over the grounds and mapped out the plans. There is no earthly doubt but that Bonnie knew all about it, too, but either Clyde wasn't taking chances with her getting into trouble any more, or else she herself had refused to have anything to do with it. At any rate, Clyde left her at his home, and he and Raymond drove away around noon. Clyde called back as he left: "Listen over the radio, honey, and see if we make our get away."

Bonnie, who was always superstitious about certain things, called out quickly: "Don't say things like that, Clyde. It's a jinx." But she went right back in and tuned in on the radio and sat down to listen. In half an hour the word was on the air. The Neuhoff Packing Co. had been successfully held up, and the bandits had escaped. They had whipped back through town, down Industrial Boulevard, thence to the West Dallas road, and picked up Bonnie, and disappeared. They went to an abandoned farm house several miles out of Grand Prairie and laid low four days. On August 5th, Clyde brought Bonnie back to Dallas to visit with me, and he and Raymond went on to Oklahoma. I knew nothing of all this till nearly a year later. All I did know was what Bonnie told me, and she didn't want me to find out what she was doing, so she told me lies.

I believe that, up to this time, even though Bonnie knew that Clyde robbed so they could live, she didn't like it and was not in sympathy with that mode of life. Clyde had never killed anyone before though the Hillsboro murder was on his head. Bonnie realized that Clyde faced the chair already because of this charge, and she didn't believe he had a chance in the world to clear himself of it. If caught, the odds were ten to one that he'd get the chair. She didn't want him caught. All of this is feminine logic of a woman in love, and has nothing whatever to do with law and order. Bonnie had become an outlaw at heart because she wanted to be with Clyde.

It was not till almost a year later, in May of 1933, that I saw Bonnie again to talk with her about any of these things, and by that time there was no going back for Bonnie either. She told me then: "I never dreamed what I was getting into, mama. I only meant to go and be with him a little while — just a few months out of a lifetime. Then I thought I'd come home and never see him again. Long before I was ready to come back home, the way was blocked, and my name was chalked up with Clyde's. It was fixed for us both — the way we'd have to go if we were to live and stay together — and death was always at the end of the road. I didn't realize, mama — I didn't realize."

I don't think, in her heart, that Bonnie would have ever come home to stay again, even if Clyde hadn't become a murderer. She loved him so madly, so insanely and so without rhyme or reason, that she would have stayed with him anyway, no matter what came. She made her little excuses to me to make me feel better, and perhaps at that particular moment she did feel that she wouldn't have gone on if there'd been any turning back. However, back to this story of August fifth.

Bonnie was up early the following morning, August 6, and seized the paper as soon as she was up. There was a story in it about the Atoka killing. Four men, said to be well known Dallas bandits, had shot two officers at a country dance the night before. One officer was killed instantly. Moore was his name. The other one, Sheriff Maxwell, died four days later. The entire affair was utterly without justification or logic, a revolting and terrible murder without any sense or reason to it. They weren't staging a hold-up and caught and forced to fight for their lives. In fact, there was no excuse for them being where they were, in the first place. It turned out that Raymond Hamilton's rather childish desire to attend a dance was what started the whole affair. Anybody with brains can easily deduce that men wanted by the law for the things Clyde and Raymond were guilty of, hadn't the least bit of business trying to horn in on a country dance. As I told Bonnie later, if Raymond just had to dance, he could have turned on the radio in the car and got out by the side of the road and hopped up and down by himself. This murder was one which roused the whole of the South against the outlaws, and with good reason.

Raymond was wanting to dance this Friday night. Cruising along the country roads, the four boys spotted the dance in progress and Raymond immediately decided that they would attend. They drove up to the place and sat awhile in their car, debating whether or not they'd better try it. Raymond was all for it. They had some whiskey and had been drinking quite a bit. They got out of their car and moved over into another car, closer to the door, still arguing. This move attracted the attention of Sheriff Maxwell and his deputy, Eugene Moore. They decided they might do well to investigate.

"What's going on here?" Maxwell wanted to know. The answer he got came from guns. Moore was killed instantly, a bullet through his heart and one through his head. Maxwell fell, badly wounded in half a dozen places. The sound of the shooting caused a riot inside the dance hall, and people began pouring out; women screamed and fainted or had hysterics; men yelled and milled back and forth uncertainly.

The four boys leaped from the car into their own and started off down the road, firing as they fled. Maxwell, on his elbow, fired after them. Seizing the guns of the helpless officers, several of the party jumped into cars and took up the chase. The car the boys were driving had a Texas license; and suddenly as it speeded down the road, something went wrong; it trembled on the edge of the ditch, turned and toppled over.

A man named Cleve Brady, who lived at Stringtown, happened to be passing, and not knowing they were bandits, stopped as any good motorist should do and offered aid. Clyde rammed a gun in his ribs and hustled him back into his own automobile, the others climbed into the Brady car, and they were off again. Outside of Stringtown about fifteen miles, Brady's car lost a wheel, and spun around in the road. Raymond Hamilton was thrown clear, but was uninjured. All four jumped from the disabled motor and ran toward a farmhouse owned by John Redden. "We've had a wreck," they told him. "A fellow down there is badly hurt and we've got to get him to a doctor, quick. Have you a car?"

Redden's nephew, Haskell Owens, obligingly backed his car down and offered to carry the wounded man to town. Before he had driven twenty feet from the farmhouse, a revolver in his side forced him to turn away from town and drive in the opposite direction at breakneck speed. A few miles further on, Clyde took the wheel. At Clayton, Oklahoma, they set Owens free in his own car and stole a machine for themselves from Frank Smith, who lived at Seminole, and disappeared.

Clyde and Raymond were not accused of the affair at first. Many were the conjectures as to who might have committed the crime. James Acker, a former convict, was picked up and held because he had a gun wound. Acker insisted, however, that bandits had held him up and stolen $7 from him, shooting him because he resisted. He had never been near Atoka nor Stringtown, and officers were unable to prove that he had been. Conjectures were at a standstill till the Seminole car was found at Grandview, Texas, on Sunday afternoon. Officers could scarcely believe the evidence of their eyes. The distance covered since the boys had let Owens go near Clayton on Saturday was amazing. But it told them one thing — the men who killed the officers at Atoka had come from Texas and had returned to Texas. I could have amazed the officers further, had I known what I know now. That distance from Clayton to Grandview wasn't covered in twenty-four hours as they thought, but in less than six, for Clyde Barrow sent to my house after Bonnie Parker at 8 o'clock on the evening of Saturday, August 6, although the Seminole car was not discovered till the next afternoon.

This was but a sample of the phenomenal driving for which Clyde later became famous. A thousand miles was nothing unusual for Clyde to cover in a day. He drove like a devil, and he had the luck of one. He also came to know all the roads in Texas, Oklahoma, Louisiana, Arkansas, New Mexico, and Missouri. Not only the main roads, but all the side roads and little country lanes. His mind was a photostatic copy of the intricate windings where he could rush in and hide, elude capture, fade into the landscape and become lost to sight.

We were again sitting on the porch, saying very little. Bonnie had planned to return to Wichita Falls the next morning, and had already ordered the taxi to call for her at five. A car drove up in front of the house with a boy in it whom I had never seen before. Bonnie ran out and talked with him a few minutes. She came back and said that she had a ride to Wichita and wouldn't wait till daylight. She gave me her bus fare, took her handbag, kissed me goodbye and left.

That was the last I was to see of my daughter for almost a year, except for two hasty visits of about five minutes each, one on Hallowe'en evening, and another on January 6th, the night that Malcolm Davis was killed. Long before Bonnie admitted to me that she was with Barrow again, newspapers had told me all I wanted to know, and a great deal that I would give my life if I could forget.

Nell Takes Up the Tale Again

During all this hectic time I had not seen my brother since the day at my mother's when I questioned him about the Bucher murder at Hillsboro. I didn't believe that Clyde had killed those men at Atoka. I didn't believe any of the things I'd been hearing and reading in the papers. This may seem ridiculous to the reader, but it's true. My mother told me that Clyde had been coming in almost every night with Bonnie, and I wanted to see him very badly. I began driving out each evening, trying to catch him, but always I got there just after he had gone. He and Bonnie were staying in the abandoned farm house near Grand Prairie, I knew, but I didn't dare go out there.

One evening right after the Atoka business my mother phoned me that she was cooking red beans for dinner, and asked me to come over. Red beans was always our code message that the kids would be in, so I drove out to the house in West Dallas and waited till 10 o'clock without success. I was alone in my car, and it was dark on that West Dallas road. A little after ten I got up and said I'd better go home. I had been driving but a few minutes before a car came up behind me and ran alongside and tried to curb me. I cut around quickly, my heart beating fast.

The car caught up with me again, and again tried to curb me. This time, in a panic, I shoved the gas down to the floor and tried to outrun the car. Again the pursuing automobile came even with me, and I saw that the driver was motioning me to turn out over the viaduct. "Fat chance!" I thought to myself, and put on all speed. Finally, seeing I had no intention either of stopping or turning off, a man with flaming red hair leaned from the other car and said, "For God's sake, Sis, you dumb egg!" It was Clyde and Bonnie.

I pulled over then, my knees still shaking, and parked side by side. "Great heavens," I gasped, "you scared me to death! I thought you were a hijacker, Clyde."

Smiling impudently, his dimple working, Clyde replied: "Hell, I am."

I climbed out of my car and started to step up on the running board, but Clyde grabbed at me and yelled, "Look out, Sis!" My nerves were badly shaken, so I jumped back, exclaiming, "Good, Lord, no! I mustn't get my finger prints on this car."

Clyde roared at that. "If you're not the biggest coward I ever saw," he told me. "Finger prints, my eye! I was yelling at you because we've been on country roads and the running board has mud a foot deep on it. Finger prints! You sound like a detective thriller." "Where in the world did you get that carrot top," I demanded. His hair was the most flaming red you ever saw.

He nodded to Bonnie beside him. "She dyed it for me," he stated. "And, boy, did she burn the hide off? I've got blisters as big as a quarter all over my scalp." "I guess I used too much ammonia," Bonnie told me. She looked very tired and worn, and was without her usual sparkle. "But he wanted it red, Nell, and he's got it red."

"He sure has," I agreed. "You can spot that a mile away."

"What I need is a wig," Clyde went on, talking very fast and trying to be funny. "A woman's wig to put on over my own hair so I won't be recognized by the law. A blonde wig would be good. Then I could pass for Bonnie's sister. Wouldn't that be a howl, honey?" Bonnie didn't answer his smile. She made a sort of snuggling gesture against his shoulder and sighed. "Nothing's very funny the way I'm feeling tonight," she said. It was obvious she was very low in her mind about something.

"Clyde," I began, "what about that Atoka killing? Were you there?"

He sobered up at that. "I was there," he agreed. "You mean — you mean — you killed those men?" I asked. "You killed them both?"

He shook his head. "I don't know," he admitted. "It's an even break whether I did it or Raymond. We were both shooting all the time."

I got sick at the pit of my stomach. "Now you've really done it," I cried. "Now you're wanted for murder, Clyde." I began to cry.

"I was anyway — for one I didn't do — the Hillsboro job," Clyde insisted. "What's the difference?"

"All the difference in the world," I told him. "You might have proved you didn't do that at Hillsboro." I hadn't a handkerchief, and the tears were all over my face.

"Not with my record, I couldn't," he said stubbornly. "The law wouldn't have believed me. I was with those boys, you know."

"But — but you might give up and just get a sentence," I suggested.

"I might give up and just get the chair," he mocked. "But I won't. No, sir, it's set now, Sis, and you might as well stop making a row every time you see me. We'll have a little while longer together — Bonnie and me — isn't that right, honey?"

Bonnie nodded her yellow head against his shoulder. "Together," she agreed.

"Atta girl," Clyde said, and patted her arm. "A few years — maybe just a few months — then —" He made a funny sound with his mouth and grinned at me. "Out — like Lottie's eye." He shifted gears.

I rubbed my face with my fist and leaned and kissed them both, perhaps for the last time — I didn't know. "Where are you going now, Clyde?"

He made an indefinite gesture. "Driving," he said. "Just driving from now till they get us. Kansas, Missouri, Oklahoma, Mexico — Texas, always Texas — where we were born. Don't look so glum, Sis. You'll be hearing from us. We'll be seeing you." He kissed me once more — for luck, he said — the impudent grin again on his face. Then, with one arm about Bonnie beside him, he stepped on the gas and took to the trail.

On August 14, we were hearing from them again, by way of the newspapers, for Clyde and Bonnie, just driving, had gone to pay Bonnie's aunt in New Mexico a visit, and had kidnapped an officer, a trick for which they later became famous. Half a dozen times within the next eighteen months

Clyde kidnapped one or two policemen and took them for all-day rides before turning them loose.

Mrs. Parker Relates This Story

Bonnie's aunt lived outside of Carlsbad, New Mexico, and when Clyde and Bonnie arrived to visit her, with Raymond Hamilton accompanying them, Millie received them with the open-armed hospitality of the farm. I noticed many stories which stated that my sister was afraid of Clyde and Bonnie and turned them over to the police, but there is no truth in this statement. I have talked with Millie about the whole thing several times and she was not aware that Clyde and Bonnie were in trouble. You must remember that this was in the summer of 1932. Clyde had been out of prison but a few months, and was not as well known then as he was before he died. Many of the robberies which were chalked up against him after his death were not placed against him at this time, and the Atoka murder was the only big thing so far. Millie lived in the country and did not keep up with the crimes of the South. Even if she had known, she wouldn't have turned them in, she told me, though she might have asked them to leave.

The whole trouble was caused by the stolen car the three were driving. They had come through Carlsbad with it and the sheriff, Joe Johns, had sighted it and become suspicious. The kids spent that night with my sister, and the next morning early — it was Sunday — while my sister was in the garden back of the house gathering vegetables for dinner, one of the boys took the car and went into town after ice. Here Johns again saw the car and noted the license number, which was the same as that of a car recently reported stolen. He got his car and followed them back to the farm.

All of them were in the house when Johns drove up, as they were getting ready to make ice cream. The guns were locked in the car, because they had not wanted to alarm my sister's family by a display of fire arms, so when the sheriff came to the door and knocked, the boys had no weapons of any sort. However, there was a shot gun in the house belonging to the men of the family.

Bonnie went out on the porch to answer the sheriff's knock, and he said he wanted to ask about the car in the yard. Bonnie replied that the boys were dressing, but would be out in a few minutes. Johns strolled back over to the car and began trying to open the place where the guns were. Clyde and Raymond seized the shotgun, ran out the back door, and got the draw on Johns before he knew what it was all about. They yelled for Bonnie to come quickly and get in the car. In the excitement, the shot gun went off, but the shot was wild and nobody was hurt. My sister said the first she knew of the whole affair was when she heard Clyde yelling: "Honey, get in the car, quick!" And then the gun went off. When she reached the front of the house, the car was already roaring down the road.

Late that afternoon Sheriff Johns was telephoning from San Antonio to tell the Carlsbad officials he was o.k. By that time, half the state was looking for him, and the body of a dead hitch-hiker had been brought in as his. However,

Johns was not hurt, and was forced only to the inconvenience of going back home where he came from, after a thousand-mile dash across the country. Johns was exhausted from his strenuous trip, but apparently Clyde was not, for the three did not stop.

At Victoria the next day they abandoned the car they had and stole another — a Ford V-8. Clyde always preferred this type of car because the steel bodies were good protection in smash-ups, not to mention their resistance under gun fire. The news of the stolen car was broadcast, also the direction Clyde had headed, and a posse of men laid a trap for them over the Colorado River near Wharton. By this time, the sedan had been augmented by a Ford coupe. Clyde was driving the coupe with Bonnie beside him, and Raymond was following in the sedan.

The officers' plan was to wait till Clyde was well onto the bridge, then the men were to rise up before him and behind him and block him both ways. The officers had not counted on two things: They had not known there would be an extra car, and they could not know that Clyde was as sensitive as a jungle cat to danger. As Clyde and Bonnie dashed down the road toward the bridge, this sixth sense of Clyde's worked automatically. Before the astonished officers could even move from their places of concealment, Clyde swung the coupe around in the middle of the wide road, swept by Raymond's speeding sedan, and headed back the other way as swiftly as he had come.

The officers leaped up out of the ground at this, all around the sedan, and bullets began to fly, but Raymond turned in this hail and flew back after Clyde in the coupe. Several officers who sought to stop him were almost run down. The officers raced for their cars and gave chase, but Clyde and Bonnie had changed to the sedan with Raymond, abandoning the coupe, and with Clyde at the wheel, there wasn't a chance of catching them. They disappeared as if the ground had opened up and swallowed them.

Clyde and Bonnie were making themselves famous or infamous, depending on the viewpoint. Their daring escapes, their breath-taking speed, the boldness with which they came and went, were becoming legends up and down the land. Pretty Boy Floyd was crowded into oblivion; Machine Gun Kelly was an also-ran. Bonnie and Clyde had the center of the stage and were to keep it till they died.

Nell Again Continues the Story

Right after the escape at the bridge, Raymond Hamilton decided he wanted to go home to Michigan and visit with his father. Clyde and Bonnie took him. This was September 1, 1932. After staying in Michigan a week or so, Bonnie and Clyde started out "just driving" again and left Raymond up there to get his visit out. The two kids drifted down into Kansas City and played around awhile, going to shows, eating at the best restaurants, having their nails done, buying some clothes. Bonnie got a permanent, too. They stayed in Michigan, Kansas, and Missouri till the last of October, and we had a great many letters from them during this time, stating that all was well. Of course, these letters were not signed.

In the meantime, Raymond's desire to dance had come over him again, and he had begun stepping out quite a bit, which would have been all right, except that he danced once too often, talked to a girl too much, and got turned in. He and a boy named Gene O'Dare were arrested and brought back to Texas for trial. Raymond's trial netted him the 263-year sentence, and he was sent to Huntsville again. He had been convicted of the Neuhoff Packing Co. job, the Hillsboro murder and various bank robberies. When Clyde heard of Raymond's sentence, he sent word that he'd get his pal out of Huntsville within a year, and he did.

By this time, every robbery, hold-up, or murder committed in the South was attributed to Clyde and Bonnie, no matter if they were a thousand miles away when it happened. Since, as Clyde had pointed out to me, he was already slated for the chair if caught, he made no effort to clear himself of charges that were not true, while, we his kin, said nothing, no matter what we knew.

Along in October an old man who kept a grocery store in Sherman, a Mr. Hall, was brutally murdered. A blonde-haired girl was reported to have wielded the death weapon, while her companion stood by. Just who did kill poor Mr. Hall is something I have no way of knowing, but Clyde and Bonnie weren't even in Texas at the time. They were in Kansas City enjoying the movies and having a breathing spell from dodging the bullets of the officers.

In fact, it was a few days after this killing, driving along through Kansas, that Bonnie turned suddenly to Clyde and said plaintively: "I want to see my mama, honey." Bonnie told me later that Clyde just swung the car around without a word and headed for Texas. Early next morning they drove past my mother's home and pitched out an empty bottle with a note in it, telling us where to meet them. That was always their signal to us if there were people around so that they didn't dare stop.

Mrs. Parker was working and couldn't get off till closing time. Bonnie moped around all afternoon because she couldn't see her mama. She announced that she was going right down on Lamar Street where her mother lived, just as soon as it was dark. Clyde was always teasing Bonnie about being so crazy over her mama, but whenever she'd get a homesick spell, he'd always bring her home if he could.

"It's the only way I can live with her, Sis," he explained. "She'll start crying and simply float me out of the car when she wants her mama, so I just put on a bathing suit and drive her in. Cops? Hell, no, I'm not afraid of them picking me up — unless they got a sight of Bonnie's face — then they'd likely pinch me for wife beating."

We asked him about the killing of the grocer, Hall, at Sherman. "We've been in Kansas for the past three weeks," he said, "so we couldn't have done that. They just hung it on us for luck. But what's the difference, now? They've got to hang it on somebody, you know."

It was Halloween night, I remember, and about dusk Bonnie wouldn't wait any longer. She said she was going to see her mama. Clyde drove her over and circled the block while she ran in. It was the first time Mrs. Parker had seen Bonnie since the 6th of August, and she saw her about five minutes, only long enough to kiss her and tell her she was well.

We didn't see them any more till after Christmas. They went up to Carthage, Missouri, and rented a tourist camp about ten miles from town. Clyde had two other boys with him now, Hollis Hale and Frank Hardy, both of Dallas. They committed minor robberies in Missouri for the next month, but were not caught or even suspected, for police were looking for Clyde and Bonnie in Texas and Oklahoma, and didn't dream they'd go so far north as this, though often they went further, clear to Michigan and Illinois.

In the last day of November they decided to rob the Oronogo Bank. Clyde told me later they had sent Bonnie in to look things over several days before. Clyde still wasn't taking her with him on any of his actual hold-ups. This time he left her about five miles out of town to wait, and he and the boys went in to raid the bank. Their finances were in a bad way, Clyde said — down to about $2, I believe — and they figured that the Oronogo Bank would furnish them enough to get by on for the rest of the winter. They left Hollis in the car out in front, and Clyde and Frank Hardy went into the bank with drawn guns.

This affair didn't turn out as expected. Evidently bank officials hadn't been so dumb as the boys had figured, and had become suspicious of Bonnie's visit. Anyway, they were ready for them.

"Gosh, Sis, they began popping at us the minute we got inside the door," Clyde told me afterwards. "We'd have beat it right then, if we hadn't needed money so bad. But as it was, I held them off and Frank made a dive for the cage and scooped up what he could get his hands on. Then we left in a hurry, let me tell you!"

The paper stated that they got $ 115, but when the money was counted, Frank insisted he had only $80. This, they split three ways and went back to the tourist camp outside of Carthage.

Immediately upon their arrival both Frank and Hollis began to make excuses to get to town, saying they'd better go and buy some ammunition. They left and never did come back, and when Clyde read the papers, he found out he'd been double-crossed. The thief had stolen from the thief. He and Bonnie had about $25 for all their troubles.

Their living expenses were always high, because they were constantly on the go, and with luck they had only enough to last a week. More was necessary, so Clyde went hunting another bank to rob. Since he must rob it alone, he was careful about the one he chose. He made elaborate scouting plans, looking over the situation, and finally selected a little bank in a small town in Missouri. Leaving Bonnie to guard the door with the car and give warning, Clyde entered the place boldly, carrying his gun.

An old gray-haired man was sitting disconsolately in a chair in the comer of the bank, apparently the only person about. Clyde said politely: "I don't want to hurt you, but I've got to have your money. Hand it over."

The old man cocked a grizzled eyebrow at Clyde and made no movement, either of surprise or terror, although a rather sardonic grin did begin to spread over his grizzled features. "Son," he said, "I wisht you'd put that gun up and stop trying to be so gol-damed funny. This bank's been closed down four days.' There ain't no money in it. That's what's the matter with it."

Clyde, whose sense of humor came now to apply to such grim things, since that was what his life was made of, related this to me with shouts of laughter when he came home again. He seemed to consider it a great joke on himself.

He and Bonnie got in this time around the first of December, I recall, because W. D. Jones, a kid Clyde had played around with in boyhood, was waiting at our house for Clyde to come in. He wanted to "go out" with Clyde, but Clyde refused point blank. " You're too young, W. D.," he said. "You stick around here where the going's good and safe. If you go out with me, you'll get in a lot of trouble and land in jail."

"Hell," W.D. exploded. "I'm in jail all the time as it is. I might as well get something out of it."

They had a big argument, but in the end W. D. went out with Clyde and Bonnie. I want to tell a peculiar thing right here. After Clyde and Raymond split up, the things Raymond wrote and said about Clyde made him furious. When W. D. got caught and started his series of fantastic stories about how Clyde chained him to trees and forced him to stay with him, Clyde was not angry at all. He'd say, "Heck, I don't blame the kid for trying to get out of it if he can. I'd do it, too." The only time I ever saw him really angry with W. D. was when Clyde thought Frank Hardy was going to get the chair for a murder that W. D. had committed himself, and W. D. wouldn't come forward and take the blame. That was the Doyle Johnson murder at Temple on December 5, 1932.

W. D. got in trouble right from the start. He was only sixteen when he started out and he wasn't accustomed to the sort of life Clyde was living.

W. D. went to steal a car in Belton this evening in December. It looked like an easy job, for the car was parked in front of a house with the keys left in it. W. D. was in the driver's seat when the door of the house opened and an old lady ran out on the porch and started screaming for help. In an instant she was joined by a man who was evidently her husband, and both of them were yelling. Clyde and Bonnie were sitting across the street in their car waiting for W. D. to get the motor going, when the old man started down the sidewalk. Clyde jumped out, and ran over to help W. D. start it, for W. D. had lost his head and couldn't seem to get it going with all the racket around him.

Bonnie, telling the story afterwards, said that just here a young man appeared on the porch, took in the situation, and ran down to the car. Clyde was on the left side, leaning in and working with the gears, and this young man — it was Doyle Johnson — rushed up to him and seized him by the wrists, pulling him around. They grappled there, the man still clinging to Clyde's wrists and yelling something to his folks about phoning the police.

"I was sure scared," Bonnie said, "and I'd have driven away if Clyde hadn't been in a jam. As it was, I never heard so much screaming and hollering in my life, and it looked like the whole town was going to be right on us in a minute. I knew it wouldn't matter if W. D. got caught, for he hadn't done anything to get electrocuted for, so I didn't worry any about him. It was Clyde I was scared about. I shifted gears and came alongside the car and called to Clyde to let the thing go and come on, quick. It was just here that W. D. let him have it. The man who was holding Clyde sort of crumpled up, Clyde jerked loose and ran around and jumped on the running board.

"W. D. followed him, and I stepped on it. Clyde was breathing hard and as mad as I've ever seen him. 'You dumb punk!' he said to W. D. 'They didn't have any guns, either of them. We could have got away without killing him if you'd used your head. Now you've got a murder chalked up against you. I ought to kick your rear till you had to ride on your stomach a week. I told you you'd get into trouble if you came along, but, damn it, I didn't think you'd do it so sudden'!"

W. D. was really scared, too. He got out of the car at Dallas and went home to his folks to spend Christmas, and a sorry Christmas he must have had. Bonnie and Clyde went to the Grand Prairie hideout, but we didn't see them till the first week in January. Of course, we didn't know anything at all about their being mixed up in the Belton business because it was not until the following spring, 1933, that the officers arrested anybody for the Doyle Johnson murder, and then the man they arrested was Frank Hardy and not W. D. Jones.

It was in the fall of 1933 that W. D. was taken into custody, while picking cotton in South Texas. At that time Frank Hardy was still being held for the Doyle Johnson murder, and it looked as if he were going to be convicted. W. D. had been traced through the pictures made with Clyde and Bonnie, which the officers found after the Joplin battle. He was brought to Dallas and confronted with these proofs by the officers. Whereupon he began to fabricate the most amazing story of his being forced to go with Clyde against his will and on fear of death; of having been constantly chained to trees and fences to prevent his escape; and of having never fired a gun during the whole time.

In fact, one of the most amusing features of W. D.'s fantastic yarn was that he was always unconscious when anything happened. He was unconscious at Wellington when he shot a woman's hand off; he was unconscious at Joplin when he helped Clyde kill two officers; he was again unconscious at Platte City; he was apparently unconscious when he helped Buck commit the robbery at Fayetteville and kill the marshal at Alma. He says he wasn't along and that the man who really did it was Clyde. Clyde was sitting beside Bonnie's bed in a tourist camp at Ft. Smith, begging her not to die, and refusing to leave her for an instant. More than that, Buck Barrow, on his dying bed after the Dexter, Iowa, gun battle, admitted before his mother, Mrs. Parker and the officers that he and W. D. committed both the Fayetteville and the Alma crimes and that Clyde wasn't even with them.

I, myself, know that every time W. D. got separated from Clyde, he'd come out to West Dallas and patrol that pike, waiting for some word from Clyde so that he could join him again. And I know, too, that when Bonnie was so seriously injured, and her sister Billie, went to Ft. Smith to be with her, W. D. was there the whole time, coming and going as free as the air, and Billie told us that she never saw a handcuff or a chain, and didn't even know that W. D. was being held a prisoner against his will till six months later when she read the story in the Dallas papers. Billie said, so frantic was Clyde over Bonnie's condition that W. D. could have walked off any time he wanted to go and Clyde wouldn't even have missed him.

These stories that W. D. told amused Clyde and never

made him mad. He said he hoped the kid put it over and got away with it. It was only this Frank Hardy business that made Clyde angry with W. D. He said W. D. was a dirty rat if he let Hardy go to the chair for something he hadn't done. I remember one night when we met Clyde and Bonnie out near Cedar Hill, Clyde asked us if we had any ink so he could make finger prints on paper. "I want to send a letter to the laws and tell them W. D. and I did that Doyle Johnson killing," he said. "If I say that W. D. did it alone, they won't believe me, for they'll think I'm trying to shift the blame, but if I say I was in on it, too, maybe they'll turn Hardy loose."

We hadn't any ink, so at Bonnie's suggestion, Clyde stuck his fingers in car grease and made prints and gave us the paper, but the prints smeared and were of no use when we got back home, so we never sent the note. However, Hardy was cleared of the charge later and it was laid on Clyde.

Bonnie and Clyde showed up in Dallas on January 6, 1933. They arrived at the home of Bonnie's mother rather early. W. D. says in his "memoirs" that he went out to Mrs. Parker's house that night and stayed quite a while, but to this good day Mrs. Parker has never laid eyes on the boy. Bonnie stayed only a few minutes, and it was evident in those few minutes that she had been drinking — something her mother had never seen her do before. The sight of her in this condition, plus the knowledge that Lamar Street was crowded with passing officers, frightened Mrs. Parker badly. She begged Bonnie to get out of town at once, saying she'd rather forego the pleasure of seeing her at all than to have her take such terrible risks. Bonnie insisted that they were leaving right away. Clyde, she said, was in town solely to see some one for the purpose of mapping out some sort of campaign to free Raymond from Huntsville. Bonnie stayed only a few minutes and left.

The first intimation we had that there had been any trouble was when the officers came to Mrs. Parker's house at midnight or a little after, and asked for Billie. They refused to tell Mrs. Parker what they wanted, but as soon as they had gone, Billie told her. Malcolm Davis, a deputy, had been shot at Lillie McBride's house and the concensus of opinion was that Clyde Barrow had done it. Knowing what she did know, Mrs. Parker was pretty sure of it. We did not get the story from Clyde's lips till the following May when we saw them again.

This is what happened: Odell Chandless, a former convict, had robbed a bank at Grapevine, December 31, 1932, and headed toward Dallas. Officers believed that he meant to visit Lillie McBride eventually, so they set a trap for him. Mrs. McBride was in Huntsville visiting with Raymond. The officers took advantage of her absence to stage a jolly little welcome for Chandless, if he should come. There were five deputies in all, and they hid around the house, waiting. The terrible joke was on them, if you call it a joke. Chandless never came, but Clyde Barrow did, and when the smoke cleared away, there was another murder to chalk up against my brother.

Clyde, Bonnie, and W. D. drove up to the McBride house just before midnight. I have already said that Bonnie had

149

been drinking, but I want to say here that Clyde had not; that he drank seldom; that I never knew him to be drunk in my life. He once told me that with his life hanging by a thread, and the constant fear of death at his heels, he would be a fool to drug his mind with liquor and lessen the chances of getting out of tight places. He also told me that Bonnie had begun drinking only after she had been out on the road with him awhile.

"I let her have at it about once a week," he explained, because the poor kid's nerves can't stand the strain. She's not built for this sort of thing, and it gets her. But I don't use the stuff much, Sis. Not from any moral sense, but from the standpoint of good common sense. I'd be an idiot to do it. No, I wasn't drunk the night we killed Malcolm Davis. The cards were just stacked against us, that's all. I walked into the trap they had laid for Chandless, and when Davis stepped out of the door and yelled 'Throw up your hands!' I swung my gun into action. I fired in the dark, and instantly four other guns began going off right in my face. The blackness was spotted with flame. I saw I was outnumbered, so I ran for it."

Bonnie was at the wheel, waiting, but not expecting any trouble. When the shooting started, she didn't know what had happened nor what to do. W. D. grabbed a gun and began blasting the landscape. Bonnie said she was drunk, but not so drunk that her head wasn't working. She reached over and grabbed W. D.'s arm. "Stop it," she cried. "You're shooting wild and likely to kill people in the houses up and down the street." She stepped on the gas and ran down the block, for the confusion was horrible, everybody screaming, and the officers still firing in the dark. Bonnie said she knew Clyde was either dead or else had made a getaway. She circled the block, and on the other side she saw him running toward her between the houses. He crawled in and took the wheel. Driving like the devil, he shot out past the West Dallas road, across Westmoreland and onto Industrial Boulevard, headed for Oklahoma, and not knowing for sure just how many were dead or dying behind him.

Clyde said afterwards that he remembered the most poignantly Bonnie's face, white in the darkness, and her voice, a little tremblingly, saying: "I won't go to see mama now, maybe never again."

"But how did you feel, Clyde?" I wanted to know. "How did you feel, knowing you'd killed another man?"

"Like I always felt — sick inside — sick and cold and weak — and a sort of dull wishing that I'd never been born. You see, Sis, it's hard to make you understand, because you've never faced it. But it comes so quickly and it happens in an instant — you're there and they're there — they've got guns and you've got guns — you know it's going to be you or them and there's no time to think about anything else. You grit your teeth and come down on it —t hey do the same, unless you beat them to it. In that case, they're telling the story and not you, next day. Then it's over and done and no going back — you've killed a man — you see him lying there, if it's daylight and you've time to wait and look. Life's gone — you took it — he'll never live and breathe and laugh again. But if he'd beat you to it, you'd be lying there like that. It gets mixed up — it seems senseless — the whole business — them killing you — you killing them — you wonder why you were born — why anybody was ever born — why God should bother with the whole mess. And you feel so helpless, so unable to do anything about it — and then you run away and get sick, and that's all."

I've tried to put it down like he told it to me, jerkingly, in little spurts, his hands passing nervously over his face as he talked. I thought perhaps it might interest people to know just how he said he felt when he'd killed a man. It interested me, for I knew if anyone else had asked Clyde what I had asked him, he'd have said: "Hell, it was them or me — why should I feel anyway about saving my own neck, except glad?" But he wouldn't talk that way to me, and I thought maybe you'd like to know what he said.

So terrific was Clyde's driving after this Davis killing, that although he left Dallas after midnight, he was far into eastern Oklahoma before the sun came up. Here they found a quiet tourist camp and rented a cottage, and here they stayed till March, not daring to come into Texas again because of the stir about the Davis killing. We received many letters from him during this period. They were never signed or dated, and were always mailed from a different town, because they were afraid that our mail was being watched. They said very little in the letters — only that they were alive and well, and we were not to worry. Not to worry! We never knew an hour free from worry. The newspapers were like death sentences each day till we read and found them to have no news of Clyde and Bonnie. We lived in constant and hourly dread of disaster; our sleep was troubled with nightmares of their death under some revolting circumstance, and my mother aged before my eyes. It was impossible not to worry, for we knew that Clyde was robbing to live, whether it was in the papers or not, and that every robbery was fraught with danger, perhaps death.

There has been much sarcastic comment — and with reason — about the fact that Clyde stole for only a few dollars here, a couple of hundred there. They did not know, as we did, that a lot of money wasn't in Clyde's scheme of things. He couldn't spend it if he had it. He was never one to have dreams of grandeur. He had no thought of making one big haul and then leaving the country, to settle down and live in splendor on his stolen wealth. He knew that he must keep on driving, till the end came, if he stayed around near home where he could see his folks, and he meant to see us. He stole only when he needed it and where he happened to find it.

It is also untrue, as newspapers and thriller magazines have stated, that Clyde stayed close to home in order to get help from us. We were a poor family. Bonnie's mother has always worked for a moderate salary. Neither of the families had anything to give them except a meal now and then, pillows when they had to live in the car, maybe some blankets and quilts, and once a pair of crutches for Bonnie when she was injured. Clyde continued coming home because he loved his people and because Bonnie cried to see her mother. I know this all sounds incongruous, but remember that even the worst criminals have families that they love. These families are human and the criminals are also human, and given to human emotions, sufferings and longings.

I don't want the reader to get the idea that we consider the things they did were right. The entire business nearly drove us crazy. After the Atoka killing, we realized that Clyde was forever outside the law and constantly in danger of death. We wanted him to live at all costs. On the occasions when we saw him, we did not spend the precious hours which might be the last we'd ever have with him, in denouncing him for his sins.

After a time the heart and mind become deadened to further suffering. We eventually grew numbed with the state of things; but I never reached the point where the shrill cry of "Extra! " late at night didn't bring me up out of my bed trembling and with the cold perspiration breaking out all over. We came to accept what each day might bring with a sort of dull apathy, shutting our eyes to the headlines, and only opening them when we could see and feel and speak to Clyde and Bonnie again. Always the shadow of sudden death stalked them; walked with them, even in our sight. We never knew what the morning and evening paper might bring.

Clyde and Bonnie talked often of death, and of how they would meet it when it came. They knew better than anyone that it was inevitable. There was nothing we could do to help them, except to love them to the last. They tried to make light of the situation to us, and insisted often that they were having a good time. Now and then something ridiculous would happen, and when it did, they made the most of it in the telling.

Such a thing occurred soon after the Malcolm Davis killing. It was the last of January, when Clyde, W. D., and Bonnie were going through Springfield, Missouri. Clyde, as usual, was driving too fast, and a motorcycle cop, Thomas Persell, took after them and chased them into the edge of town, finally forcing them to the curb. Then he racked his motorcycle and came around to the side of the car to demand, in the eternal formula of speed cops: "Where's the fire, buddy?"

Clyde grinned at him and began opening the door. "Down the block a piece," he said. "Let's take him, W. D."

W. D. was out in a flash from the back seat, and before the surprised Mr. Persell could figure out what was happening to him, his gun had been lifted, he was hoisted up unceremoniously and dumped into the back of the car, and a blanket thrown over him. Then W. D. climbed in and put his feet on him and covered him with his own revolver. "Just going for a little ride," Clyde explained, and started his car.

So quickly had they acted that nobody had seen them. They drove calmly away and left the motorcycle as mute testimony that its owner was missing. All night long people searched frantically for Officer Persell, who was by that time 200 miles away, having made stops at such towns as Buffalo, Fairplay, Golden City, Carthage and finally Oronogo, where they were forced to steal a new battery for their car. At Poundstone Corner the three bade Mr. Persell a hilarious farewell and let him out.

By that time the officer was as mad as a wet hen, and aware that his plight was rather ridiculous. It was noon of the next day before he could telephone Springfield. He reported that he had been riding with Clyde and Bonnie and an unidentified man. Also, that Bonnie had dyed her hair red. This affair was printed in the papers, and it was the only report we had from them for quite awhile.

My brother, Buck Barrow, was pardoned from Huntsville on March 22. The pleas of my mother and the intervention of Buck's wife, Blanche, had managed it for him. I had been going down to see Buck often while he was in Huntsville, and he certainly appeared to be a changed man. He told me he'd never do anything to get in trouble again as long as he lived; that he meant to go straight now, and make a home for Blanche.

He had worried about Clyde constantly during his stay in prison. It had been his job to sweep out the cells and generally clean up each day. He told me that he never swept around that terrible electric chair but what he thought of Clyde. "I used to dream at night that Clyde had been caught and brought to the death house," he told me. "I'd wake up in a cold sweat. I couldn't have stood it if that had happened while I was there. Something has got to be done to make Clyde straight with the law again, Sis."

It was all fantastic, for Clyde was forever beyond being straight with the law again. Soon after he came home, my sister gave Buck the money to buy a secondhand car. Buck was going to Missouri to visit Blanche's people and probably go to work on the farm. Buck had never had a job in his life, as I have said. He didn't know how to do any sort of skilled labor, and he just wasn't attracted to work, anyway. We had the highest hopes of his trying to stick to a job now because of Blanche.

He hadn't been home but about four days till he began talking about going to visit with Clyde, if he could find him. Blanche was bitterly opposed to it. Newspapers have made Blanche out as a regular gangster's moll, but nothing was ever further from the truth. She was a good country girl, timid, shy, and rather quiet. I suspect if she'd known Buck was an escaped convict when she met him, she'd be running yet instead of serving time in a Missouri prison. Buck didn't tell her till after she married him, and then she brought him right back to serve his time, as I have already related. Blanche had never been in trouble with the law in her life, and she was deathly afraid of guns, bloodshed, and any sort of outlawry. She was afraid of Clyde, too, and she didn't want to visit him then or at any other time.

Buck had never used a gun, either. Unlike Clyde, who loved his guns, named them all and spent hours cleaning and polishing them, Buck had never owned one, and was, I'm inclined to believe, scared of them himself. His record had been for petty thievery, not for murder or holdups. Even officers taunted Buck with being a coward.

I didn't blame Blanche for kicking about going to find Clyde. I told Buck so. I said: "You fool around with Clyde, and you'll land back in the pen with a life sentence. You haven't got the nerve and daring to do the things that Clyde does and get by. You'd get caught right off."

Buck laughed. "Listen, Sis," he said, "I'm no fool. I wouldn't ride a block with Clyde. I know what it would mean. But I haven't seen him in two years and I want to visit with him. That's all I'm going to do — just visit with him. Now don't you worry, Sis. I'll be back, safe and sound."

He came back safe and sound, all right — in his casket.

Blanche cried two whole days before Buck left. She kicked up a terrible row, and looked as if she had lost her last friend. I wasn't very happy about the situation, but I'd given up trying to change either one of them by this time. Buck came by my shop that morning and told me I'd get a telephone call from an unknown man. When this person called I was to say: "He's already gone."

They drove off with Blanche still boo-hooing. The man called and I delivered the message. A few days later word came that all was well. Buck and Blanche had met Clyde and Bonnie just outside of Ft. Smith, Arkansas. They had gone on to Joplin, Missouri and rented a house in the suburbs, one with rooms above and a double garage below. Here they were having a quiet time, just being together. Clyde and Bonnie, having been away from home for three months, were eager for the news. They talked a lot. They cooked red beans and cabbage, of which Bonnie was so fond, and which were never cooked to suit her in cafes. They read magazines; Blanche, her fears calmed a little, played solitaire, and romped with her little white dog; Bonnie wrote some new verses and copied some already written. They sent their laundry out; had their cleaning done; and the girls mended and darned. All in all, it was just the usual family reunion, with the exception that Clyde was wanted for three or four murders, which, of course, sounds incongruous.

I've always been glad that they had these few weeks together before they got into such desperate trouble. Blanche went against her will. She was always scared to death. She never wanted to do any of the things she did do, and she never really did anything except sit by and weep and beg Buck to take her home. Her only crime was that she was caught with the Barrows. At this time being with the Barrows was a crime.

When funds began getting low — their combined finances were down to $8 — Clyde decided to do something about it. He took W. D. and started scouting for a place to stick-up. He didn't tell Buck where he was going, but he did tell Bonnie. After he reached the car, he came back and kissed her again. "I hate to leave you, honey," he said.

"Big silly," Bonnie laughed. "I'll be here when you get back."

"It's not that," Clyde told her. "But I've got a hunch something's going to happen." I told you he had a sixth sense. He could sense danger before it came. He was full of that feeling this morning — so much so that he hadn't gone a dozen blocks before he wheeled the car around and went back. "I can smell it," he told W. D. "It's in the air. We're not scouting this morning."

He ran the car in the garage and locked the door, and just

as he did, the officers arrived on the drive outside. Upstairs in house slippers and negligee, Bonnie was preparing to take the red beans from the fire and put in the corn bread to cook. Blanche was playing solitaire, the dog asleep at her feet, and Buck was lying on the couch, dozing. "It's the law, Bonnie!" Clyde yelled.

Bonnie said afterwards, the things which stood out clearest in her memory concerning this gun battle was the fact that she could smell her precious red beans burning, hear Blanche screaming and running, and the dog barking wildly. Then the guns began roaring all around her. Bonnie grabbed a gun, ran to the window and fired. "But I know I didn't hit him," she insisted. "He ran off down the street. Then before I could fire again a slug came through the top of the window and glass shattered all around me. Buck shoved me down, yelling, 'Get back, for God's sake!'

"Down in the garage W. D. and Clyde were spraying the landscape with their machine guns, and Clyde was yelling commands to me above the awful racket: 'Get down into the car — you and Blanche — get in the back of the car!' he called, never stopping with that deadly machine gun. 'Lie down out of sight — no, take the guns with you, Bonnie — never mind anything else — I'll be along. Run! For God's sake, honey, run!'

"I ran, but there was no Blanche to go with me. Frightened to death, she had jerked the door open at the first shot and gone down the stairs, screaming with terror and fear, the little dog behind her. They were both a half block away. Without waiting to change into dress or shoes, I fled down and into the car. I remember Buck had a gun as he came down the steps but I don't recall his shooting any. Lead was flying all around us, splattering into the walls, sinking into the doors, shattering the windows. Buck and I got in the car. W. D. had been hit in the head, and just as Clyde started to climb into the front seat, he looked down and saw blood streaming from his chest. I remember he stood there a second, gazing down, then whipped back his shirt and said: 'Can you find it?' meaning the bullet. I probed the hole hastily with my finger tips, felt the flattened bullet, and with Clyde's help and a hair pin, pulled it out. It must have bounded back from the wall and struck him, because it wasn't in deep. Clyde swore furiously and ran around the corner of the garage with his machine gun. When the seconds seemed hours, I went hunting for him. The guns were still cracking and popping. I found Clyde squatted behind the corner of the garage.

" 'For God's sake,' I cried, 'come and get in the car.'

" 'Not till I get the dirty rat that shot me,' he replied. 'Get the car out and going.'

"About that time a deputy stuck his head around the corner and Clyde let loose, blowing a big hole in the wall. Whether or not this was one of the officers later reported killed, I don't know. I only remember that I pulled Clyde's shoulder and he shook me loose and ordered me to get the car out again.

"I ran back to the car. Buck had got the door open but the officers' car blocked our escape. W. D. ran out and released the brakes on the other car and gave it a shove. It ran down the drive and across the street, careening into the curb. I remember seeing it skidding around crazily, and that there was a man, all bloody and moaning, lying on the drive in front of us. W. D. started our car, but Buck grabbed his arm and yelled: 'You'll run over that man!'

" 'Hell, who cares?' W. D. cried. 'The dirty rat!'

"'I'll move him,' Buck said, and darted out in the hail of bullets and dragged the dying officer to one side. Clyde staggered around the garage just then, running. The firing had never let up an instant. It was hell. I'd never lived through such hell. Every minute seemed like it would be our last. Clyde was wounded, W. D.'s head was spouting blood, Blanche was gone, and the shells were still spatting and snarling at us. Still firing with one hand, Clyde slipped under the wheel and we roared down the driveway. W. D. was taking care of his side of the car with another machine gun. I tugged at Clyde's shoulder and pointed. 'Blanche went this way,' I yelled above the din. Clyde nodded and turned down the street.

"We found Blanche two blocks away from the house. She was still running and sobbing, her face white as chalk and her eyes popping out of her head with fright. The little dog was in her arms. She got in with us in a sort of dazed, numbed way, and sat in the back seat with me. I had W. D.'s head in my lap and was trying to stop the blood which poured from his wounds. Blanche still had the deck of cards gripped tight in her hand, and after I had got W. D. fixed up — I bandaged his head with a piece torn off his shirt — I tried to get those cards out of her hand. I had to work for thirty minutes. The poor girl was petrified with fear, and kept whimpering pitifully: 'I want to go home — I want to go home!' Well, didn't we all?"

Driving like an insane man, Clyde was rolling into Amarillo in less than eight hours, where medicines were purchased for W. D.'s wounds. The officers of three states were now wanting not only Clyde and Bonnie, but Buck and Blanche, and an unidentified man as well. Identification of the first four had been easy, for the group had fled, leaving everything behind. Blanche's purse contained Buck's pardon and their marriage license, and several roles of films, which after being developed, proved to be snapshots of four of the wanted fugitives. In this group was the one of Bonnie, with the cigar in her mouth and the gun on her hip, which was to brand her forever as Clyde Barrow's "cigar-smoking gun moll." Other pictures which particularly outraged the Missouri officials showed various members of the gang posing with Officer Persell's stolen gun. Being dumped in the back end of a car and carried out of town under a blanket had not appealed to Mr. Persell's sense of humor, although Clyde and Bonnie had considered it a great joke. When one remembers the dead men Clyde had already left behind him, I suppose Officer Persell should have been glad that the situation made him only ridiculous and not a corpse. The big man-hunt was on. Both my brothers were being tracked down like animals, and neither would be given the slightest chance, nor shown the least mercy when caught.

Buck's chances of becoming a regular citizen were now

gone forever. The chair was waiting for him, also. You can well imagine that ours was not a happy family during this period. We seldom spoke the names of the fugitives, and if someone mentioned them, another would hastily change the subject. Talking would do no good. We knew nothing about them except for a few hastily written words bidding us not to worry and not to believe all that we read in the papers.

They were constantly on the road during this time. Kansas, Louisiana, Missouri, Texas, Oklahoma, New Mexico, Iowa, and Illinois — there was never any telling where a letter would be postmarked. They avoided tourist camps and never slept in beds, living, eating, sleeping on the road, often going sixty miles an hour for hundreds of miles before stopping. They camped along little used country lanes in dense underbrush, sleeping always in relays so that someone would be on guard to call out and awaken them.

W. D.'s wound healed in time, with the doctoring they could give it, and so did Clyde's. Neither wound was deep or severe. Their laundry and bathing presented the greatest difficulties. They were particularly sensitive about cleanliness, and Clyde wanted his suits always cleaned and pressed. Often they suffered acutely between washing and bathing days. Getting a bandit's family wash done was a ticklish job. They would usually leave the clothes in some small, sleepy little town, then drive on for a couple of days, circling back to get it. Getting it was the dangerous part. They never knew whether they had been recognized and a trap made for them for their return. Such was their standard of cleanliness that they placed themselves in this danger week after week, in order to be decently clothed.

Since they were denied the use of showers or tubs, bathing was more difficult. When it was freezing weather, they would often find a stream and take turns standing in the icy water with a cake of soap, hastily scrubbing themselves of the accumulated grime of several days, returning to the car, blue and shivering, and dressing while the winds whipped around them. Often they were cold and stiff for hours after these baths. The boys shaved in wayside streams in cold water, and got haircuts in small town barbershops while someone stood guard in a car in front, ready to blow a signal on the horn if danger threatened.

Their food too, presented a problem. Restaurants were denied them, and supplies were purchased in small, isolated towns where the choice was limited to pork and beans, canned soups, cheese and crackers, and canned meats. Bonnie, who loved red beans and cabbage, had little enough of them during these days, for beans take time to cook, and they did not dare make a big fire or keep one going long. Clyde also had to forego his favorite drink, hot chocolate. Occasionally Bonnie would concoct it for him out of canned milk, but he liked it with whipped cream and oceans of marshmallows, which were unobtainable in the places where they shopped.

On the Wednesday after Mother's Day in May, 1933, Blanche came riding into Dallas on a bus. This may have seemed a foolhardy thing to do, considering the Joplin affair and the two murdered officers, but remember that

Blanche was not known to the law, and they never had a picture of her till they took one the day she was captured at Dexter, Iowa. She was perfectly safe. She took a taxi and came out to my mother's house. She told us where we were to meet the kids.

We had not seen Bonnie and Clyde for five months, nor Buck since he went to find Clyde. There was a great deal of excitement in the Parker and Barrow families. The usual message about red beans was telephoned and we made ready to go. We were all nervous, eager, and scared to death — so much so that we overlooked taking any food with us, and the whole crowd spent the day without a bite to eat.

While we got the clan together for the trip, Blanche went into town and shopped for some riding boots and breeches, and very nice and trim she looked in them, too. We were to meet Clyde, Bonnie, and Buck near Commerce, Texas, on a country road where there was a bridge over a ravine.

I don't think there was ever a visit filled with so much happiness and sorrow. We had lived through a million hells since last we met, and we had no assurance that we should ever behold their faces again in this life. It was a great deal like visiting those in prison condemned to die. We knew that death was coming eventually, as surely as the sun rose. But we could not know when.

We tried to be gay and nonchalant, and to gloss over the horror of the happenings in the past five months. There were times when we succeeded in laughing merrily over the stories they related to us. Clyde teased Blanche about her newly purchased boots. "They'll be awfully hard to run in, Blanche," he told her. "And running is one of your best accomplishments." Then he related her flight at Joplin with the deck of cards and the dog.

If it seems bizarre and fantastic to the reader that we should laugh about these things, please remember that such happenings were all they had to tell us, and that we had to laugh or burst into hysterical weeping. In fact, I kept an eagle eye on both my mother and Mrs. Parker during the whole day, dreading just such an occurrence, and we headed it off by strategy more than once. Both mothers were suffering; the nerves of both were ragged, and both were heart-broken, graying, and older looking by years.

Blanche retaliated for the dig about running away by re-lating to us the big spat Clyde and Bonnie had had recently. Bonnie had gathered all her clothes and put them in a pa-per sack and marched off down the road, "going home to mama," she said.

"You should have seen old Clyde's face," Blanche laughed. "It was a study. He hadn't an idea that Bonnie really would leave him. They started fighting about something — I don't remember what, it was such a little thing — and the row grew and grew till Clyde told her to shut up. That finished matters. Bonnie told him to stop the car and let her out; she was going back to Dallas if she had to thumb it all the way. Grinning all over his face, Clyde stopped the car, and out Bonnie got, gathered up that paper sack and started marching away down the road.

Clyde sat there and laughed and laughed, thinking Bon-nie would come back, but she didn't. Pretty soon he started honking the horn; then he yelled at her. Bonnie kept right on going. When Clyde started the car up to catch her, she turned into a corn field and went running down the rows, still lugging that sack of clothes. Buck and I just howled, which didn't help matters. Honestly, it was the funniest thing to watch him chasing Bonnie up and down those rows, begging her to come back, and to hear her answering that she'd never do it — she was going right home to her mama!

"Finally, Clyde caught her and such a fight as they had. He picked her up and brought her back, kicking and scratching and crying. The paper sack was torn and her clothes were scattered from one cornstalk to another. Buck collected them, because Clyde was too busy holding Bonnie in his lap and trying to get her to make up."

"Let him try to get smart again and I will, too, come home to my mama," Bonnie said.

"You try it, old sugar, and if the law doesn't kill you, I will," Clyde promised. But he kissed her as he said it. He knew, just as we all knew, that he'd never have to kill Bonnie for leaving him because she wasn't going to leave him.

Another story that set us off into gales of mirth was Clyde's yarn about buying red beans for Bonnie. "We'd stood up under canned stuff as long as we could," Clyde said, "when one day we were driving down a country lane and our noses told us that somebody was cooking red beans inside. Red beans and corn bread. Bonnie said she just had to have them, so I got out and went in and asked the farmer's wife if she'd sell us some. She immediately started setting the table and urged me to bring Bonnie right in and draw up a chair and set, but I told her no, we just wanted the beans, not the whole dinner.

"She kept insisting and I began to get nervous for fear some of the men folks would come in from the fields and recognize us, so I said firmly: 'No, thank you. Just give me a half-gallon jar full of those red beans and I'll pay you whatever you think it's worth — a dollar — two dollars. We'll take them with us.'

"She looked like she thought I'd lost my mind," Clyde went on: "She was still standing there in the door looking that way when we drove off, Bonnie hugging that jar of beans like it was full of gold dust. And boy, did we eat beans! We were both stuffed like pigs when we finally downed the last bean, but we never enjoyed anything as much in our lives."

Blanche, still smarting from the ragging she'd evidently been getting ever since the Joplin affair, told us one on Bonnie then. It seemed that during the night of the terrible hail storm in March, the two girls had been left parked in the car on a deserted road all night long. Buck, Clyde, and W. D. had gone to get some money — I believe they were going to rob a bank somewhere, only it didn't come off. At any rate the two girls were left all night in the car alone. Hail and thunder and lightning came, followed by a terrific downpour. Bonnie, who was always afraid of a storm, had hysterics. She covered her ears, she put her head between her knees, she wept and she moaned and prayed, and begged for Clyde or her mama. She said she knew they'd both be killed and never live to see day again. "In fact,"

Blanche said wickedly, "she behaved much worse than I did in the Joplin battle. She got down on the back seat at last and made me pile all the pillows and blankets on her head, and then she wanted me to sit on top of them! I never heard such goings-on as Bonnie did that night. I felt sorry for her, but I had to laugh. The idea of not being scared of bullets flying right and left, and then yelling her head off at a little hail."

"I was scared at both places," Bonnie interrupted. "Only at Joplin I knew I was going to be killed if I didn't run, and in that hail storm I couldn't run. I just had to sit still and let it hail."

It was during this day near Commerce, which passed all too quickly for us, that we got the particulars of the Malcolm Davis killing, the Doyle Johnson murder, the kidnapping of Officer Persell, the New Mexico kidnapping, the trap on the bridge at Wharton and the Joplin battle. Also the story of the kidnapping of the undertaker, D. D. Darby, and his girl friend, Miss Sophie Stone at Rushton, Louisiana, on April 27, soon after the Joplin raid.

"Our own car was sunk, and we were practically afoot," Clyde told us. "Darby's car was sitting out in front and we went and climbed into it. We were just driving away from the curb when Darby and Miss Stone both popped out the door, looking rather surprised. W. D. waved his hand and said, 'Thanks for the buggy ride.' Then we beat it.

"Darby didn't mean to let us get away with it. He jumped in Miss Stone's car, she came along, too, and they started chasing us. But Darby was afraid to drive as fast as we were going. Near Hico, they began falling behind and finally turned around and started back to Rushton.

"'Let's go take 'em,' I suggested, for a lark. We'd been chased so much, it was a new experience to start chasing somebody else. We turned around and took in after them. Boy, were they scared when they saw us coming! Darby did his best to outrun us, and it was really pitiful how frightened they were when we finally caught up with them and ran them to the side of the road. But that wasn't anything compared to how white they turned after they got in the car with us and found out who we were. We didn't realize till then how the name of Barrow could frighten people out of their wits. We never intended harming them and we never did do them any hurt, but we certainly got the slant of the other person during that ride. We learned that all the South was scared to death of us, and that officers would no more think of trying to take us single-handed than they'd think of jumping off Washington monument. Later, we learned this was true by experience, when they came after the five of us with posses 200 strong, armored cars, and steel shields, and enough machine guns to have stopped the Germans at the Marne.

"The going was pretty crowded with seven of us in the car, so we didn't keep them long. At Magnolia, Arkansas, we gave them $5 expense money and put them out about 8 o'clock that night. The fun we'd had with them had been worth more than $5, but we didn't happen to have any more to spare just then."

Other robberies credited to them following this, were

not true, Clyde said. They did not rob and brutally beat the filling station attendant at Broken Bow, Oklahoma. Neither did they rob the filling station in Fort Dodge, Iowa. They did hold up the First State Bank at Okabena, Minnesota, on May 16th. That was the place where the whole town turned out to catch them — they committed the robbery in broad daylight — and Clyde was amused at Bonnie because she wouldn't shoot an old man who tried to wreck their car as they dashed down the square.

"Blanche refused to have anything to do with any robberies," Clyde told us, "so we had to leave her out of town waiting for us. The three of us went in and Bonnie stayed in the car in front of the bank. We locked the people in the vault and got away with $2500, but everybody in town seemed to know about the hold-up before we did, and there was a regular reception committee waiting for us when we came out, everybody shooting right and left. I was driving with Bonnie beside me ready to hand me freshly loaded guns; Buck was in the back seat, and I couldn't depend on him to do any shooting, so when I saw this old man running out toward us carrying a great big log — he was on Bonnie's side of the car — I said, 'Honey, shoot him before he wrecks us.'

"Bonnie just sat there, and when I saw she wasn't going to do anything, I had to jerk the car away over to one side to keep from hitting him and the log, which he tried to throw under our front wheels. I almost turned the car over. 'Why in the name of God didn't you shoot him?' I demanded. 'It's a wonder we weren't all killed^'

"'Why honey, I wasn't going to kill that nice old man,' Bonnie told me. 'He was white headed.'

"Well, I felt like I was white headed too, before we got out of that town, and I told Bonnie that nice old man would have just loved to see us lying cold and dead, but she didn't seem to mind that part at all. I'm not trusting Bonnie to shoot any more than Buck after this."

In spite of Clyde's joking, the thing he was most worried about, and about which he spoke most often, was the spot Buck was now in because of the Joplin fight. Clyde blamed himself for Buck's predicament. He said over and over: "And just think — they had planned to leave us the next morning! I still believe if Buck had used his head and run downstairs with both hands up and surrendered, he'd be all right now. I think he could have told them that he was just visiting with me and had nothing to do with the things I'd been doing. I think they'd have believed him and let him go if he'd done that."

"Things happened too fast for me to figure that out," Buck explained slowly. "You don't think good at a time like that. Suddenly the cops were there and everybody was shooting and running. I didn't think — I just ran."

Clyde talked it over with us all rather soberly before we left. "Suppose Buck goes back in with you tonight and you call the cops over and tell them the whole truth," he said. "Tell them Buck never fired a shot — that W. D. and I did it all — don't you think they'd believe him?"

Buck, after thinking this over while Blanche watched him tensely, shook his head at last. "No, they wouldn't believe me," he said. "They might if I didn't have a prison record already, but I have. I'd get the chair, Clyde. It's no use. I've got to stick with you now — the four of us together till they get us, I guess. Don't take it so hard, kid." Blanche was crying and I saw my mother was ready to break down. It seemed a good time to turn the conversation elsewhere. Besides, it was getting dusk.

We had spent the whole day parked on the bridge, for there had been a heavy rain the night before and the roads were terribly muddy. I remember that Clyde had to back his car off the bridge every time anybody came along. We stayed in the cars almost all day, except for a little while when Bonnie and her mother walked down the road for a talk. I didn't hear what they said, but Mrs. Parker told me afterwards she had been trying to persuade Bonnie to come in and give up before it was too late.

"You'll get only a prison sentence if you come in now," Mrs. Parker explained. "And while that's bad, still and all, it's nothing compared to what may happen before this is over. You're not made for this sort of life, Bonnie. The strain is going to kill you if a bullet doesn't. I'd be happier with you in prison than like you are, honey."

Bonnie wouldn't hear to it. "Clyde's name is up, mama," she said. "He'll be killed sooner or later, because he's never going to give up. I love him and I'm going to be with him till the end. When he dies I want to die anyway. Let's don't be sad. I'm in as big a spot as Clyde is. My name's up too. And though it may sound funny to you, I'm happy, just being with Clyde, no matter what comes."

We came home very soberly and quietly. None of us there that day were ever to see Buck and Blanche again till we met over Buck's deathbed in Iowa, and visited poor timid little Blanche, who was so afraid of guns. I think all of us prayed on that homeward trip. I know I did. I prayed that they'd stay out of trouble and live a few years longer. They were so young to die. Buck had only two more months to live, and Bonnie and Clyde had but a year.

As for their staying out of trouble, I guess it wasn't in the cards. It was only a month until they were in headlines again. Bonnie was lying at death's door in a tourist camp in Ft. Smith, Arkansas, in her delirium begging and crying for her mother who dared not go to her. Those are the untold tragedies of the relatives of fugitives. We dared not go to them when they had need of us — for fear we would reveal their whereabouts.

Immediately after this meeting near Commerce, Blanche and Buck slipped away to Missouri to visit with Blanche's parents. Bonnie and Clyde took to the road alone, and we had no news of them for several weeks. During this time W.D. Jones showed up at my mother's house. He said he had become separated from Clyde and Bonnie in Oklahoma. He went to steal a car, an officer had spotted him, Bonnie and Clyde ran for it and he'd beat it back to Dallas. Now he wanted to know where Clyde was and how he could find him again.

This was along about the first week in June, the 8th, if I remember correctly, because when the story about the accident in Wellington broke on June 1 Oth, an unidentified man was again with Clyde and Bonnie. He had shot off a woman's hand in a farmhouse near Wellington. That sounded about like W. D., who always had an itchy trigger finger. I telephoned my mother. "That couldn't be W.D., could it?" I said. "He's still in Dallas."

"Oh, no," my mother replied. "Clyde came after him yesterday. They've gone to meet Buck and Blanche. That's where they were headed when the accident happened."

For a week we had no way of knowing anything except what the papers told us. Then Clyde came for Billie to be with Bonnie when she died, and when Billie came home we heard the whole story.

Clyde, Bonnie, and W. D. were speeding along over the West Texas roads, headed for Erick, Oklahoma, where they were to meet Buck and Blanche. I told you that Clyde always drove like a devil. He was making about 7 0 miles per hour. A bridge was out and he didn't see it till it was too late to stop. They hit the place, turned over twice, and rolled to the bottom of the ditch, with Bonnie pinned underneath the car.

Clyde, thrown clear, pulled W. D. and the guns out. Then the car caught on fire. The flames were all around them and Bonnie began screaming and begging them to do something for God's sake, and if they couldn't do something, to shoot her. W. D. said Clyde seemed like an insane person, who couldn't feel fire. He kept going back into the flames, tugging, swearing, and crying as he worked. About this time two farmers rushed up from the fields. "Help us," Clyde begged them. "For God's sake, help us."

Between the four of them they got the burning car off Bonnie and lifted her out. She was horribly burned, her face blistered, her arms badly seared, and her whole right leg a mass of cooked flesh. She was in great agony, too. Newspaper reports stated that Clyde threw a gun into Pritchard and Carter's (Editors's Note: Instead of Carter, this was actually Alonzo Cartrwright) ribs and demanded that they carry Bonnie up to the house. Both Clyde and W. D. told us this was not true. "With Bonnie hurt like she was, would I be fool enough to start brandishing a gun?" Clyde demanded. "Hell, no. Those newspapers make me sick, always looking for some wild story. All I was thinking about was getting relief for the kid. I didn't know that she was hurt as badly as she really was. I thought the women up at the farm house could fix her up. My only trouble was a car to get away. I figured I could get one somewhere after they'd made Bonnie comfortable. Common sense would tell you, Sis, that at a time like that I had nothing to gain and everything to lose by brandishing a gun.

"The men helped me carry her up to the house, while W.D. stayed behind to cache the guns, because I thought we'd be needing them later. Up at the farm house Mrs. Pritchard put mentholatum on Bonnie's face. When she begged for something on her leg to ease the awful pain, Mrs. Pritchard looked at the seared flesh and shook her head. 'I'm afraid to put anything on that,' she stated. 'That needs a doctor.' She did put wet baking soda on her arms though."

All the while everybody was insisting to Clyde that they

must get Bonnie into a hospital at Wellington at once, and were wanting to call an ambulance. Clyde begged them not to, and Bonnie in the midst of her terrible pain, added her voice to his pleading, for she realized as well as he did what it would mean. This refusal to send for medical aid when Bonnie was obviously so badly hurt, made the Pritchards suspicious. "Do what you can for her yourself," Clyde said. "I can't do anything more," Mrs. Pritchard replied. "She needs a doctor and she needs one right now."

Clyde ran out of the house, back to the burning car, and gathered up the guns. He didn't see any car about the farm-house, and he was at his wit's end. Bonnie must be taken away immediately, but how? While Clyde was gone, Carter slipped out of the room, and at that W. D. whipped out his gun. I don't know whether he did it because he was afraid or whether he just liked to have a gun in his hand. He began brandishing the weapon and threatening to kill Pritchard because Carter had left. Mrs. Pritchard screamed and Mr. Pritchard protested that he had done nothing except be friendly and try to help. W. D. admitted this and subsided, the gun still in his hand. Bonnie's moans could be heard all over the house, and Mrs. Pritchard, despite her fears, never ceased doing what she could to help her. "They were so kind to me," Bonnie told us. "So very, very kind, and I was hurting so and wanting mama, and scared, too."

It was just at this moment that the door began opening, and W. D. whirled and fired. There was a feminine scream from the other side, and Mrs. Jack Pritchard, a relative, stagged into the room with her hand shot away. W. D., appalled by the mistake, saw there was nothing to do now but hold them all off with his gun till Clyde returned. Just how this was going to end was something none of them could figure out. Bonnie, despite her suffering, had leaped from the bed at the sound of the shot, and rushed into the yard.

Carter had slipped away and telephoned officers at Wellington. Their car was even now swinging into the farm house road. Clyde, down at the burning car, heard the shot and came on a run with the weapons. He took in the situation at a glance. Delay was unthinkable. There was only one way to get out of there alive and that was in the officers' car. He pulled W. D. into the hedge which grew around the house, threatening the Pritchards with instant death if they made any sound or gave warning. "These people aren't armed," Clyde said to W. D. "We'll take the officers."

They crouched and waited, while the policemen came in through the back and out onto the porch, walking carefully with drawn guns. Then Clyde and W. D. sprang at them, seized their arms, pinioned them against their sides and handcuffed them with their own handcuffs. Taking their guns from them, the two boys marched the men helplessly toward their own car. One was put in the front seat. W. D. and the other went in the back, and Clyde lifted the moaning Bonnie and laid her in their arms.

"You hold her easy," Clyde commanded. "Don't you let her hurt any more than she's got to hurt. Sorry about that hand, people. Let's go." They tore down the road and onto the highway, headed for Erick, Oklahoma, Buck and Blanche.

It hurts me yet when I think of the agony that Bonnie must have suffered during that terrible ride, without medical attention, without a bed to lie on, without any opiate to ease her horrible pain. I'll say this for her: Right or wrong, she was the gamest, grittiest little kid that ever walked; she had only one ruling passion in her life now — love for my brother; she knew that he would get her aid as quickly as he could, and that he could do no more than he was doing, unless he gave both himself and her up to the law. Bonnie would have preferred any sort of death rather than see Clyde caught. She had said so, and her actions on this occasion proved it conclusively.

After three hours of this terrible drive, they met Blanche and Buck outside of Erick. Here W. D. took barbed wire from a fence, and he and Clyde tied the two officers, whose names were Corry and Hardy, to an oak tree. Buck came over and watched the proceedings. Blanche was already in the car trying to make Bonnie more comfortable. "Are you going to kill 'em, Clyde?" Buck asked.

Clyde grinned wryly through the soot and grime on his blistered face. "No," he said. "I've had them with me so long I'm beginning to like them." The truth of the business was that the officer in the back seat had held Bonnie so tenderly and so carefully that Clyde said he was almost ready to kiss him for it. But Corry and Hardy knew that they had been kidnapped by the desperate gunman, Clyde Barrow, and it would never do to have them go back to the world with the story of a big softy who had got maudlin with two laws.

They drove away, leaving the officers, who freed themselves within thirty minutes, and telephoned Wellington. The scent was strong now, and fresh; the hunt was on again in earnest. Everybody knew that Bonnie was horribly, perhaps fatally burned. Tracing them was going to be as easy as picking out a red dress in a daisy field. But it wasn't.

Why they didn't discover them is still something 1 can't understand, for Clyde's usual cleverness deserted him. He became like an insane man. He had only one thought: Bonnie. She was unconscious most of the time now, but apparently in great pain. Her burns had never been dressed and it was imperative that they be attended at once if she were to live. Throwing caution to the winds, Clyde took the wheel of Buck's car and never slackened his pace of sixty miles an hour till they sighted Ft. Smith, Arkansas. Here he rented a double cabin, explaining to the manager that his wife had just been badly burned by an oil stove explosion at their camp site. He sent boldly into town for a physician, and when the doctor arrived, examined Bonnie, and announced that she must either go immediately to a hospital or have a nurse, Clyde got the nurse. He'd have hired a dozen nurses.

He never left her bedside, day or night, for a week, but sat beside her, holding her hand, talking to her, pleading with her to live, putting pillows to ease her, trying to get her to take nourishment, lifting her up and down as if she were a baby. Bonnie in her delirium called again and again for her mother, begging and pleading for her till Clyde nearly went crazy. Finally the doctor said one morning: "You'd better send for this girl's mother, if she wants her. Otherwise, she'll probably never see her daughter alive."

Clyde asked for another doctor and there was a consultation. Neither physician held out much hope. Clyde made up his mind then. He came to Texas openly and alone, making no effort at concealment. He left Ft. Smith at noon on Sunday, June 19, nine days after the Wellington accident, and driving like lightning over those hundreds of miles, he arrived in Dallas at 8 o'clock that same evening, and told the horrified Mrs. Parker the condition that Bonnie was in. Both Mrs. Parker and Clyde's mother immediately made ready to return with him, but Clyde refused to take them. "I'll take Billie," he said, "but not you two. Don't you realize the cops are watching your every move? Don't you know they'd follow you and find us? No, I'll take Billie."

Billie was at a picture show and they had to wait till she came in, which was around eleven o'clock. During those three hours, the two mothers used every known persuasion to get Clyde to change his mind, but without success. "They'd jail you if they caught you," he said. "I've got plenty on my head already, but I'll never have it said that I was the cause of getting my own mother or Bonnie's mother in trouble. Maybe Billie and I can get out of town without being caught, and if Bonnie's got to die, she'll have her sister with her. But she can't die — Oh, God, she can't die — she can't — she can't!"

Then Clyde Barrow, "the toughest egg since Jesse James," Clyde Barrow, the desperado who had already killed three men, broke down and sobbed like a little boy. It broke our hearts to hear him. Bonnie's horrible plight broke our hearts. No matter what he had done, he was ours and we loved him, and how could we fail to love the girl who had cast her lot with his for better or for worse, knowing all the while that it could never be better, and who now lay at death's door in a tourist camp, begging for her mother who dared not go to her?

Clyde and Billie left at midnight. By daybreak they were back in Ft. Smith, but Bonnie didn't recognize her sister for days. She had a high fever, was delirious, and unable to sleep or rest except under the influence of opiates. Billie stayed with her constantly. She told us that during the seven days she was there, Clyde never left Bonnie's bedside for longer than five minutes at a time.

Funds were beginning to get very low, for doctor's fees were cash and so were nurses' wages. Medicine to dress Bonnie's burns cost as much as $5 for one day'* dressing. Bonnie would insist on the bandages being changed half a dozen times a day, hoping vainly that the changing would bring relief. She recognized Billie on the third day, and after that, began to improve slowly. It was seven months before she was able to walk normally again, despite the many newspaper stories which had her running everywhere with Clyde in just a few weeks. Many, many weeks Bonnie never moved from the back seat of the car without being lifted out, and it seemed that no sooner would the leg begin to heal than something else would happen to tear the wound open again. In September, 1933, which was the next time we saw them, Bonnie still walked with the aid of crutches, and had to be helped in and out of the car.

Billie stayed with Bonnie from Monday, June 20, till the following Sunday, June 26. Because of the low state of their finances, which Clyde wasn't bothering about, Buck and W.D. went out to get some funds. Police credited them with robbing the Alma Bank on June 22, and taking $3,600. The hold-up sounded like Clyde, all right, because it was so daring. Two bandits kidnapped the newly elected Marshal of Alma, Mr. Humphrey, carried him inside the bank and tied him to a pillar. Then, holding the employees off with guns, they trundled the safe out on the sidewalk and loaded it into a truck, where they headed for the Ozarks, presumably. Both Buck and W. D. insisted that they did not do this hold-up, and it seems likely that they told the truth. If they got over $3,000 on the 22nd, it doesn't seem rational that the next day they would stick up two Piggly-Wiggly stores in Fayetteville for a paltry few hundred. The Alma haul, if Buck and W. D. had made it, would have been ample for them to have lived on for several months, and with Bonnie so badly hurt, all they wanted was enough to get along till able to travel again.

Billie said their funds were so low when it came time for her to go home that they did not have enough money to buy her a ticket on the train without leaving them flat. They brought her down to Sherman and put her aboard the train there. It doesn't seem logical that they would have come back into Texas — all of them crowded into one car and Bonnie still so sick — unless they had been forced to do so. With over $3,000 in their pockets, they could have afforded to send Billie home much easier and with less worry to them all.

They did stick up the Piggly-Wiggly stores in Fayetteville on the 23rd, and on this occasion their car number and their descriptions were broadcast; also the fact that they were headed toward Alma, fifty miles away. The outraged and humiliated Marshal Humphrey heard the descriptions and decided that this was the pair who had tied him up the day before while they lifted the Alma Bank safe, so he took his car, and with a deputy named Salyars accompanying him, started out on the highway to head the bandits off.

Driving along the road, a friend named Wilson sighted them. Wilson was coming from the opposite direction, and he started to draw up for a chat, but Humphrey saw another car tearing down the highway behind Wilson and yelled at the man to keep going or pull over else he would be wrecked. Humphrey speeded up, but not in time. The oncoming car crashed into Wilson, and automobile parts were scattered all over the highway. Wilson was not hurt but he was pretty mad. He climbed out of the wreck, picked up two rocks and started at Buck and W. D.; Humphrey was about a hundred yards away and couldn't see what was going on in Buck's car. He did see Wilson stop suddenly, let out a yell of terror, and start running the other way as fast as he could. He never came back.

Rather amazed at this peculiar conduct on the part of his friend, Humphrey alighted and started back to investigate. Perhaps the occupants of the other wrecked car were seriously injured. Coming closer, he recognized the license number, whipped out his gun and yelled, "Throw up your hands!"

Both Buck and W. D. came out of their car shooting, the open doors on either side serving as a shield. Buck had a forty-one; W. D. a Browning automatic. Buck's fire went wild, but W. D. was a better shot. Humphrey fell, a hole in his chest, and Salyars was left alone to face the two of them. The deputy's own account of this fight states that the shot from the forty-one went over his head, but that the man with the shotgun had better aim and he thought he was done for till he heard a harmless click and realized the gun was empty. W. D. reached inside for another gun just as Salyars fired, but the deputy's gun was also empty. Salyars ran and no one can blame him. Reloading as he scurried out of danger behind a barn, Salyars took up the fight again, but without success.

Buck and W. D. saw their chance and ran for Humphrey's car, which was the only one left that would go. Once safe in the car, they speeded down the highway. Seven miles down the highway, Humphrey's car blew a tire. The two boys took a car from a passing motorist, and drove on into the hills near Winslow. Officers were jubilant when they heard this. They had the outlaws trapped at last, for they had followed a blind road into the hills. The stolen car, deserted a few miles further on, made them sure that the bandits would soon be captured. Posses poured into the mountains, looking for them. The trail seemed hot when they came upon a Mrs. Rogers, who stated that two men had beaten her with trace chains because she wouldn't give them the keys to her car. Buck told us she gave them the keys without any trouble, but that in trying to back the car down out of the trees, they ran it against one and ruined it. They went on afoot.

All night long men with guns and torches scoured the hills looking for Buck and W. D., who had calmly dropped back to the highway and caught a ride to town with an unsuspecting farmer, taking vegetables into Ft. Smith. Back at the tourist camp, Buck and W. D. said they had a wreck on the highway and ruined their car. That's all that Billie learned, though they must have acquainted Clyde with the whole affair. They wanted to leave the camp that night, Billie said, because the law was likely to come to check up about the wreck, but Clyde refused to go, saying that Bonnie was not yet able to travel. However, the next night they did prepare to leave. There was a great deal of stir about the murder of the Alma Marshal, and I'm sure that Clyde knew by now just what had happened. To remain longer meant serious danger for them all, but more especially for Billie, who would be implicated if they were caught.

The six of them now had only one car, a turtle back, and there was no time to get another. Clyde had Billie get in the front seat, then he lifted Bonnie up into her lap. Blanche was concealed in the turtle back with some bedding. W.D. and Buck were left at the camp to complete the packing, while Clyde took the girls up into the hills to a secluded spot. Here Billie made as good a bed as she could for her sister while Clyde drove back to the tourist camp and picked up the other two boys. When they were all together again, Clyde told Billie to get her things ready, for he was taking her back to Dallas. The trail was too hot and the danger too great. He dared not let her stay any longer. He took W. D. with him in the turtle back and went looking for another car. They found one in Enid, Oklahoma, a doctor's car, and it had a complete medical kit in it which was to come in handy later. They abandoned the turtle back. Billie told us they had three blowouts on the way from the tourist camp to the hills on the first trip. Fixing a blowout with the knowledge that bullets may start singing over your head just any minute is rather a nerve racking business.

Sunday night, June 26, Clyde, Buck, Blanche, Billie and W. D. left the mountain hide-out and started for Dallas. At Sherman they gave Billie her train fare and left her. They headed back toward Kansas where they rented a tourist camp at Great Bend, and settled down to wait for Bonnie to get well. Clyde was the only doctor Bonnie had now, and she said that he was as gentle and tender as a woman, dressing her burns as often as she demanded. She was getting better, and as convalescents are prone to do, crosser and more exacting. They lived quietly. Clyde was more worried about Bonnie's condition than the condition of their finances, letting W. D. and Buck attend to those matters. Proceeds from the robberies were small, and only enough to live on. They also ranged in a wide circle in order not to attract the law to their hiding place. Our letters from them bore postmarks from all over Kansas, Iowa, and Illinois, for Buck would mail them when he and W. D. were "out."

The reader can easily understand the state of mind we were in, especially Bonnie's mother. We knew that Bonnie was still badly hurt and should have the best of medical attention. Fear of blood poison or tetanus was constantly in our minds. We also knew that they were liable to be "jumped" any day and all killed.

It was a terrible month, during which we could only hope and pray.

The attitude of local police did nothing to soothe Mrs. Parker's mind of worries. They came to her, soon after the Wellington accident, and said: "They'll find your daughter on some lonely road now with a bullet through her head. A man as hard, as cruel, and as heartless as Clyde Barrow is, will never put up with a wounded girl who is a dead giveaway and a burden to him. You'll see."

The officers were wrong in their estimate of these hunted people. Many of the things they said of Clyde were true; but he had his code of love and loyalty. Bonnie had placed her life in his hands; she had thrown her lot with his till the end should come; she loved him as devotedly, as passionately, and as blindly as any woman ever loved a man. She had proved it again and again.

Where Bonnie was concerned, Clyde was as gentle as a baby, as tender as a mother. He once deserted her at Kaufman, before the trials of the trail had shown him her great love, but during those last two years Clyde would have died a thousand deaths rather than to have hurt Bonnie. He himself said to Mrs. Parker a few weeks before they were killed: "I'd give my life if I could bring Bonnie back to you just as I took her from you — young and carefree, and without a price on her head."

About the middle of July Bonnie was able to travel, but

she could not walk, and had to be lifted from the back seat at every stop. Her leg was drawn up under her from a burned ligament, and it didn't look as if it would ever be straight again. They drove to Ft. Dodge, Iowa, on July 18th, and robbed three filling stations. Bonnie, still in the car with bandages on her face and arms, was with them for the first time, and through her they were identified. A few days prior to that a farmer found a camp site in the woods with bandages covered with blood, so it was reasonably certain that Clyde and Bonnie were back on the trail again.

With officers everywhere looking for them, and their pictures glaring from every newspaper and bill board, it is amazing that they would dare to rent a tourist camp in this region. That is what they did. Immediately following the Ft. Dodge holdups they arrived at the Red Crown Tourist Camp, six miles out of Platte City, Mo., about 10 o'clock at night, and took a double cabin with a garage between. Newspaper stories stated that Bonnie rented the camp and was identified by her bandages. Blanche rented the cabin, but Bonnie's name made a better story.

Blanche went out that night and bought five suppers and five bottles of beer, which she took to the cabins. Bonnie was also credited with this. Not that it matters in the final estimate, for Bonnie had done and was to do many things worse than renting tourist cabins and buying suppers for outlaws. I'm simply telling what really happened. The fact that Blanche had red hair, and that she paid for her purchases in small change, plus the tightly drawn curtains in both cabins, aroused suspicion. There was a secretive air about the whole crowd. The men stayed shut in and did not show themselves.

Bonnie had to have more medicine for her burns and Clyde said that he would get it. They were all travelling in one car. Clyde didn't want to lessen the chances of their get-away while he was gone by taking the car. He got out on the highway and hitch-hiked into Platte City to a drug store where he bought bandages and medicine. It was getting dusk. He bought some papers and hitch-hiked back to the Red Crown, generally known around Platte City as "The Junction." Blanche brought in the suppers, they ate, Clyde dressed Bonnie's burns, and they went to bed. It was still early.

Meanwhile, stories that Clyde and Bonnie were at the Junction were all over town. The Platte City officers were afraid to attempt to take them alone. Clyde's name now was one to strike terror into every policeman's heart, and Buck's was about as bad because of his association with Clyde. Besides, Clyde was considered a sort of modern Fu Manchu, able to appear and disappear at will, leaving death behind. Officers were taking no chances with this gang, and certainly one can't blame them. Stories had asserted that Bonnie was a crack shot, as well as Blanche, and that both girls would enter into gun battles with gusto. Clyde had taught Bonnie to shoot, all right, and she had done some shooting on several occasions, but Blanche had never handled a gun and was still scared to death of them.

Platte City police had no intention of being the central figures in a swell bunch of funerals, so they called the sher-

iff of Jackson County at Kansas City, and asked for rein-
forcements. It was ten o'clock before the Jackson County
officers arrived with an armored car, some steel shields,
and plenty of machine guns. Bonnie had been put to bed
and was asleep. Clyde, who always slept lightly, had dozed
off. Blanche said she was still awake, but that she could hear
Buck snoring softly. I don't know about W. D.

The first intimation that they had of trouble was when
the officers pounded on Blanche's cabin and said they
wanted to talk to her. W. D. blamed Blanche afterwards
for what she did, but I didn't. The girl couldn't help being scared to death. She called out tremulously that they'd
have to wait till she dressed. All the time, she said, she was
throwing things into the handbag, just why I don't know,
unless she thought she'd better pack up for a trip. The officers pounded again and said they wanted to talk to the
men. Then Blanche yelled: "They're not here — they're in
the other cabin." Buck jumped to his feet at this, and she
put her hand over his mouth, but Clyde had already heard.
He leaped up fully clothed, opened the door to the garage,
flung the guns into the car, and said to W. D. "I'll bring
Bonnie — you take the wheel, kid." But again they were
trapped by a police car outside on the drive.

Clyde aimed through the garage doors and let loose a
blasting fire from his machine gun, riddling the car outside, and injuring one officer, Ben Thorpe, in the knees.
This direct hit through the officers' armored car changed
their minds about staying where they were. They backed
away from the garage, which was just what Clyde wanted.

W. D. ran and pushed the doors open, Clyde shot through them and W. D. jumped on the running board as the car went by. They emerged into a perfect hail of bullets. The darkness was sprinkled with spurts of flame. Clyde answered, firing with one hand; W. D.'s gun was going full blast. Several officers fell. A chance shell struck the horn on the armored car and short circuited it. It began to shrill wildly. The concealed policemen thought this was some sort of signal for help and rushed into the open to fight.

The way was open, but Clyde dared not leave. Buck and Blanche were still in the cabin. He had no way of knowing whether they had been killed or not. "I'll have to go after them," he shouted to W. D. Just at this moment Blanche staggered out, half carrying Buck. He had been shot twice through the head, and was unconscious, blood flowing from his wound. Blanche dragged him a few feet in that withering fire, and collapsed with him. "I can't do it," she screamed. "He's dying."

Clyde leaped from the car and ran to her recue. Between them they got Buck into the back seat with Bonnie. Blanche held him in her arms. Lead was pouring all around them in a stream, striking the machine, and their return fire was punctuating the night with flashes of fire. Clyde leaned low, shot the gas to the engine, and they roared through the barrage toward safety, the posse scattering as they came on. Bullets crashed through the windows, and Blanche screamed once, high and clear. They all heard her. She pitched forward over Buck's limp form, blood streaming from her face and her eyes blinded. There was no time to stop and attend the wounded.

Fifty, sixty, seventy! The speed indicator leaped up like a living thing. The pursuit was hot behind them. Telephone and telegraph wires hummed and buzzed with warnings, but the officers again miscalculated. They thought Clyde would try to go through Platte City and they concentrated their enforcements there. Clyde was no such fool. He cut out his lights and drove on in the dark, found a country lane, cut into it, and lost the pursuit.

Buck was still unconscious and Blanche was moaning constantly. Something had to be done for them. They turned off the country road into a field and stopped the car. They had nothing on which to lay Buck except newspapers, but they spread these out and lifted him from the car. Here in the glare of their headlights, Clyde saw for the first time the awful thing that had happened to Buck. The bullet had entered one temple and plowed through to the other. He could not see and was in great pain. The doctor's kit was called on for all it had. Hydrogen peroxide was poured into the wound — the worst thing possible, physicians said afterwards — and the head was bandaged.

Clyde knew his brother was in a serious condition and should go to a hospital at once, yet a hospital meant death in the end. Blanche, her eyes cut by flying glass, could see but dimly and was suffering a great deal, though her wounds were not serious.* They had nothing to put on her eyes except a pair of dark sun glasses to shield them from the light. Clyde did. bathe them with water from a nearby stream. Buck was still bleeding slowly. Blanche's dress was a mass of blood. They discarded it in the field where all these things were later found bearing mute testimony to the seriousness of their condition. Bonnie was unhurt, but badly shaken and frightened. They drove on in the night, not knowing where to turn nor what to do.

* *Four operations have been performed on Blanche** eyes in the Missouri prison, and she is able to see out of only one of them.*

By daylight Clyde had covered many hundreds of miles with his car of wounded people. Buck was running a high fever, and Blanche was in constant pain. The car held a horrible cargo of agony and death, and Clyde was half frantic about his brother. Again they were forced to stop. Bonnie's leg was causing her great suffering and needed dressing badly. Clyde wanted to make another attempt to do something to give Buck relief from the torture he was undergoing. Once more they left bloody bandages beside a country road. They did attempt to burn these, but a passing car frightened them so that they ran away and left them half-consumed.

They had had no food, and they dared not stop to buy any. Buck asked constantly for water and they had none. Buck's delirious ravings and pleadings were driving Blanche to insanity. She said she knew Buck was going to die unless he went to a doctor, and she wanted him taken to one. She didn't care what happened to the rest of them. Clyde tried to reason with her and show her that either course meant death, and that she would suffer a million times more if they took Buck in and let the state heal him so they could kill him in the name of justice. Blanche was past reasoning. She was in such pain herself and so wild with grief and love that she raved crazily. Buck regained consciousness during this tirade. He added his voice to Clyde's.

"We won't give up, honey," he muttered. "We keep on driving."

"But you're going to die," Blanche sobbed. "I'd rather we'd both spend the rest of our lives in prison than to have you die, darling."

Buck managed a weak grin. "I hadn't," he said. "I've been in jail, you see. You haven't. Besides, jail isn't what they'd give me if I got well. No, we keep on driving."

They kept on driving . . .

By late afternoon Clyde saw that they must stop. The crowded condition of the car with three wounded people was beyond human endurance. He turned into Dexfield Park, a plot of ground covering some twenty acres lying between Dexter, Iowa, and Reddings. Here they drove till they found a secluded spot hemmed in by dense woods and underbrush on all sides, and with a river nearby for water. Clyde and W. D. got out and made a bed for Buck, and one for Bonnie. Blanche refused to lie down, but insisted on sitting beside her husband's bed. She asked the others not to mention her injury to Buck, and it was easy to keep the news from him, as he could not see well himself.

The first consideration was for medical aid and food. They had had nothing to eat for two days. Clyde went into town for both, taking W. D. with him. They drove to Perry where W. D. stole another car, a sedan. They must have two cars if they were to travel with the invalids. Clyde also bought alcohol to sterilize Buck's wound and some sedative to ease his pain. He purchased five chicken dinners and the two returned to the hide out.

Here they stayed for three days. On the morning of the third day death was on Buck's face. Clyde began to pack. "Where are we going?" Bonnie asked him. "We aren't going anywhere," Clyde told her. "I'm taking Buck home to mother."

"You aren't going without me," Bonnie said. "And why should you drive all that way to take Buck back? You know he's dying, honey. He'll be dead by night." "I'm taking him back because he's dying," Clyde replied grimly. "I promised mother — we both promised her — for that matter, I promised your mother, too — if either of us died or was seriously sick, the other was to take him home. I'm keeping my word, that's all." Blanche moved over to Clyde's side, feeling her way along. "I'm going too," she said hoarsely. "I'll never leave him, no matter what comes."

W. D. had nothing to say to all this. He was roasting weinies over the fire. Clyde had stacked the guns and cleaned them the night before. For some reason W. D. had no gun on him, and Clyde had only a pistol. The odor of the roasting weinies filled the air. Buck stirred and asked for water, and Blanche hurried back to him. It was early morning; things smelled good and fresh; the woods were quiet, and the only sound was the river, and some birds in a tree above the camp fire. Bonnie looked up and saw the officers coming toward them. Newspaper accounts vary as to the exact number — some say forty, some say two hundred. The woods seemed alive with them. Suddenly bullets were whizzing and screaming through the leaves, spattering into the camp fire, striking the cars and clipping twigs from trees. Bonnie screamed. Clyde snatched a machine gun and began firing; W. D. dropped his weinies and seized a machine gun too. The possemen broke and ran for shelter at the first blast from the other guns.

"Get in the car," Clyde yelled. "Quick — get in one car, everybody." Clyde was always master of any situation.

Bonnie, who hadn't moved without help for two months, found herself running to the car unaided; such is the healing power of fear. Blanche kept trying to put shoes on Buck's naked feet so he could walk in the thorns. "Let his shoes alone," Bonnie screamed. "Come on." She could hardly see — poor Blanche — she kept fumbling with Buck's shoes. At last she got him on his feet and started dragging him along toward the car. Bonnie helped her in with him. Clyde and W. D. were busy with their machine guns; they didn't dare stop and help. The instant they were all inside, Clyde jumped in and started the motor and tried to make a getaway, but before he'd gone a dozen yards, a bullet struck his arm, he lost control of the wheel and ran the machine up on a stump. He and W. D. got out and tried to pry the front end off the stump with their machine guns, but it was useless. It wouldn't budge.

"The other car," Clyde yelled. "Pile out — for God's sake, pile out!"

Bonnie helped Blanche again with Buck. They ran for the

other car. Buck fell twice. He was shot in the back. Buck-shot had spattered Bonnie all over her body, but she said afterwards she didn't feel them at all — didn't know she was hit till she looked down and saw her dress was red with blood. W. D. received another head wound and the blood was pouring down his face.

Clyde's arm was bloody and useless. They reached the other car, but the possemen beat them to it. They riddled the car from rear axle to front fender. In five seconds there wasn't a window left in it; two tires were shot away; gas poured from a dozen holes in the tank. Buck fell again. "Take Blanche and run for it," he cried. "I'm done for anyway. Run for it."

"I'll go and get another car," Clyde promised. "Hide — they can't find you in these thickets. I'll get back."

"Take Blanche," Buck begged, but Blanche was down beside him with no intention of leaving.

"Take care of Bonnie, W. D.," Clyde said. Then he dived into the underbrush. Bonnie and W. D. dashed into the woods. The guns of the possemen redoubled their volume now. Buck kept begging Blanche to go, but she wouldn't. She crouched down beside a stump for shelter, and pulled Buck's bloody head over on her lap. Bullets struck him again and again — he had five wounds in his back when they took him to the hospital. Why they didn't kill Blanche is beyond comprehension. She began screaming at them above the noise:

"Stop, for God's sake, stop. Don't shoot any more — you've already killed him."

"Make him throw up his hands, then," someone called, and Blanche answered them with a burst of tears:

"He can't throw up his hands — he's dying."

They closed in then, warily, stalking their prey and not trusting Buck. I don't blame them. Horrible as the whole thing was, I still don't blame them. In their place, I'd have been scared to death, too. I still dream of Buck lying there, that awful hole in his head, while bullets thudded into his defenseless back, Blanche sitting there, holding his head in her lap and begging them not to shoot him any more. I do blame them for tearing Blanche away from Buck, with her begging him, "Daddy, don't die — don't die — don't die!" I blame them for locking her in a prison and refusing to let her see him before he died. He lived only six days, and asked for her constantly. It couldn't have hurt anything to let her be with him in death, after the way she'd stood by him in life. I find it in my heart to understand or make an attempt to understand the attitude of the officers and the public about almost everything concerning the criminal careers of my two brothers, but I say this freely and without compunction: Their conduct on this occasion was subject to criticism. They could have acted with more human feeling and lost nothing in the final accounting, for Buck was beyond their holding now, and Blanche was safely in the hands of justice. But it's all over now, and who am I to ask for justice?

Bonnie told us so graphically of their escape that I shall try and set it down as she related it later.

Bonnie Tells of Their Escape

Clyde left us, running through the woods toward a house over the bridge where he thought there might be a car. Because Blanche and Buck stayed behind, they were off our trail for awhile, and we had a chance to crawl away and hide. W. D. was blinded by blood, but he helped me as much as he could. We had no guns — nothing with which to defend ourselves. We knew we were lost if caught. I was bloody from head to foot, and briers and thorns had torn my bandages away and the burn was open again. Blood ran from my leg at every step. We came to the river and stopped. We crept back into the underbrush and crouched down. The firing had died away. We knew they had captured Buck and Blanche — that was why we had been able to get away. The minutes dragged like hours. Every sound was like a footstep. Even little lizards running over leaves made my heart stand still. I didn't know where Clyde was, how he'd find us, or where we'd go if he did. Clyde could always do the impossible, but I didn't believe he could get back into the park with a car. I didn't believe it was possible — not with the woods full of officers.

Suddenly the firing broke out again, louder and closer. The air was filled with the noise of it, men shouting and running, pistols popping, the rattle of machine gun fire. Then it was still again. I knew they'd got Clyde. My heart turned to ice. Nothing else mattered — my wounds — my leg — death — nothing. They'd got Clyde. We lay there in the leaves quietly, neither of us moving. At last, after a long time, W. D. said: "They got him this trip, Bonnie."

I said: "I wish I had his gun, that's all."

"You couldn't do any good with it," W. D. told me weakly, his head lying in a pool of blood.

"I could do all the good I wanted to do with it," I replied. "I could kill myself. He's finished and I don't want to live." I began to cry. W. D. reached out and patted me on the shoulder clumsily and said, "Don't, kid, don't."

Again we lay there a long time. We heard a rustling in the underbrush and a soft hiss. We lay like dead people, we were so scared. Soon the soft hiss came again. W. D. wanted to answer it but I wouldn't let him, for I was afraid it was only a ruse from the cops to get us to break cover, so we lay still and said nothing. After a long time it came again, close now, and then, crawling on his all fours, his arm hanging useless, his clothes soaked with blood — he had four bullet wounds — Clyde came toward me. I just lay there and looked at him, and all the world became the most beautiful place I'd ever known.

"Are you all right, honey?" Clyde asked me softly. I nodded. "Are you all right?" I asked.

"I'm o. k.," he said. He sank down beside me in the leaves and slipped his good arm under my head and kissed me. We lay there and clung to each other and never said a word for a long time. It was the happiest moment I'd ever known in my life, and nothing else mattered now. We were together again.

"I got a car all right," he whispered finally. "But they were waiting for me at the bridge. They wrecked it so I couldn't cross, and they almost got me. But we'll get over the river and get one. Can you make the river, kid?"

W. D. said he could. We crawled down the river bank and waded into the water. There wasn't much use of any of us trying to help the other, for we were all in a bad way. I had no idea we'd ever get away alive and I didn't care. Clyde and I were together. We left bloody ripples behind us as we swam.

Midway in the stream the posse sighted us again and the bullets began whizzing overhead and plunking in the water. Something struck me in the shoulder. I remember screaming and going under. When I came to, W. D. had me on his back and we were coming up the bank. The guns were still blazing on the opposite bank and Clyde had nothing to fire back with, for his pistol was water soaked and useless. We could only run. We had one advantage. The river was between us now, which was something.

Clyde left W. D. and me in the cornfield and went on up to a house on a hill where three men were standing on the porch watching the fight. Using his useless gun to frighten them, Clyde got the keys to their car. He whistled to W. D. and we came out of the field. Clyde made two of the men lift me off W. D.'s shoulders and put me in the back seat. I remember feeling the seat cushion beneath my face and hearing one of the men say to Clyde: "She's dead." Then I lost consciousness and when I came to it was dark, and W.D. was at the wheel, driving at breakneck speed. Clyde was moaning in the front seat beside him. I wanted to get up and help Clyde, but I couldn't. I passed out again, and then it was daybreak. W. D. had stopped the car somewhere in Iowa down a country lane beside a little stream. We were as bloody as slaughtered animals and had no clothes to change to. Obviously, we couldn't be seen on the highway like we were.

We got out and crawled down to the water and washed ourselves as best we could. Then I took off my dress and the boys removed their shirts. Lying on my uninjured side, I washed the blood from them by soaking them a long time in the clear cold water. We lay there, saying nothing, while they dried. Clyde was awfully sick. His arm was useless and was paining him. The other wounds were hurting, too. W.D., with the luck of one charmed, had only a scalp wound. He was better off than either of us, and the only one able to drive. We put our clothes back on when they had dried. We felt we must get out of that part of the country as quickly as possible, and decided to head toward Denver.

We stole a newer and better car at Polk City, Iowa, the next day, for speed was imperative. Clyde, concealing his wounded arm, swung his useless gun on a filling station attendant and took what money he had. We had neither clothes, money, nor guns. We took to the road again. Our wounds still bled, but we had neither medicine nor bandages and we didn't dare stop to buy any. Newspapers stated that Clyde tried to get a doctor and bought a hypodermic in Dennison, Iowa. This is untrue. We weren't in

Dennison. We were headed for Denver. We drove all day Wednesday, and on Thursday we were almost to Colorado City. W. D. stole a newspaper from a country mail box. It said I was in Denver in a hospital seriously wounded. The trail was too hot. We dared not go on. We turned and ran for it once more.

Where we went I don't recall. We lived in little ravines, secluded woods, down side roads for days that stretched into weeks. We were all so sick that time went by without our knowing it. We lost track of the days. Eventually our wounds began to heal. W. D., sick of the whole business, left us as soon as Clyde was able to drive again. We learned that Buck was dead and that Blanche was in prison. We knew our people must be frantic with worry about us so Clyde and I started to Texas soon after that. It was the middle of August. We felt that the end of the trail was near and we wanted to be close to home when death came out to meet us.

Mrs. Parker's Story of Buck's Death

When word came over the wire that Blanche and Buck had been captured and that Bonnie and Clyde had escaped, horribly wounded, my heart stood still. I felt that they had crawled away to die. I craved to learn all news of them. When Clyde's mother, and his younger brother, L. C., started to drive to Perry, Iowa, Billie and I went with them. We left home at 1 o'clock on Tuesday morning, drove all that night and arrived at the King's Daughters Hospital in Perry at noon Wednesday.

The place looked like an armory. Guns fairly bristled about it. Perhaps the reader will doubt me when I tell the precautions that were being used in Perry to assure the officers that Buck was going to stay in that hospital, although he was plainly unable to get out, and had no place to go if he did get out. He had but four more days to live. The great doors of the hospital were barred; his door was securely locked and only nurses and doctors went in and out. Officers stood guard at the hospital doors; officers patrolled the halls; officers sat on the back porch. I know this, for I spent most of my visit there, trying to learn from them what I could concerning the Dexter battle. I was frantic for news from Bonnie and these men had seen her last. I talked with the men, too, who had helped Clyde put her in the car when they fled, after swimming the river. These men assured me she couldn't be alive — that she was like one dead when they lifted her from W. D.'s arms.

I learned many surprising things from these officers. They attributed supernatural powers to Clyde Barrow. Despite the factual evidence of their own eyes as to the desperately wounded condition of Clyde and Bonnie, these men — and all the rest of Perry — were positive that Clyde was likely to return any minute and snatch Buck from his hospital bed right under their very noses. A constant ripple of terror was over the townspeople; the very name of Barrow was a crawling fear. It would have been laughable if it hadn't been so tragic. Buck was dying; Blanche was in prison; Clyde and Bonnie, when last seen, were bloody and half crazy with pain, Clyde with a useless arm and Bonnie unable to walk. Yet they expected them back to rescue Buck Barrow — from what? The grave?

Billie and I rented rooms in a house across the street from the hospital. When we went over to the place that night, we were escorted by a police guard, whether for their safety or ours, I could not know. The woman who owned the place, after a whispered conference with the officers, came upstairs and asked me if I wanted to lock myself in, or would I prefer that she lock the door on the outside? I replied that if there was any locking to be done, I'd use the key, since I didn't relish being on the second floor of any building and unable to get out the door. She went back and again conferred with the officers. She turned on the front and back porch lights so that the house was a blaze of electricity. Billie became nervous because of all these precautions and wanted to go back to the hospital and sit up all night, but I was tired and worn out. No matter how insane the rest of the town seemed to be about the Barrows, I was going to get some sleep.

When we came downstairs Thursday morning, the woman who wanted to lock us in was waiting for us. "I was scared to death last night, Mrs. Parker," she said. "Weren't you?"

"What was there to be scared about?" I inquired.

"I thought the kids would come back," she whispered.

I hadn't had any coffee yet, and the strain of grief and worry made my temper rather short. Her attitude seemed silly and I had little patience with it. "What kids?" I demanded tartly.

"I mean — Bonnie — and Clyde," she whispered, glancing hurriedly over her shoulder as she spoke, as if she expected them to pop out on her with a machine gun at any minute.

"They're probably lying dead somewhere in some ravine," I told her grimly. "And if they're alive, why should they come here to be shot at again?"

"Oh, they'll come and get Buck away from the officers," she insisted. "Everybody thinks so. Even the police. They put extra guards around the hospital last night. They're expecting them."

"And just what," I replied, "would Bonnie and Clyde be wanting with Buck, knowing he's dying?" She shook her head knowingly. "They're expected anyway," she said.

The constant and heavy guard proved that they were, but we weren't expecting them.

Although Buck had recognized his mother and brother when they arrived Wednesday, by Thursday his mind was wandering and he became confused. L. C. was Clyde to him; Billie became Blanche. He kept begging Clyde to run — run — and take Blanche with him. He'd be quiet only when his mother or Billie held his hand. I remember when we started to lunch, Billie was sitting there holding his hand, and his mother said: "We're only going to get something to eat. We'll be back, Buck."

"Take Blanche with you," he begged. "Don't leave her.

"Blanche isn't here, honey," she replied.

"Please take her — she's hungry," he muttered. "Poor little Blanche — take her with you, mother." Knowing where Blanche was and her sad condition, it was no wonder that his mother broke down in the corridor and wept.

He grew steadily worse, raving for Clyde and Blanche all day Friday. At 2 o'clock on Saturday, July 29, Buck Barrow died. We prepared to bring the body back to Dallas.

The law had never once relaxed its vigilance where we were concerned. Guards still paced up and down; police followed our every move, even when we went out to make funeral arrangements. The officers had told me that they were sure Bonnie and Clyde were hiding in a vacant house on the edge of town. They kept constant watch on it, they said, and no one came or went. I asked an officer why they didn't go in and find out if they were there. He made some evasive reply, but I knew the answer: They were afraid.

I said: "Good heavens, if they're in there and you're watching the house, and nobody comes or goes, it stands to reason they're dead. Why don't you go and find out?"

They didn't, though. Instead they put police on our trail to follow us out of town, thinking we'd go by if they were really there. They seemed to believe that Clyde used mental telepathy to communicate with us, or sent us wireless messages. How they figured that we could hear from them, I don't know, since we were under police surveillance from the day we arrived till we departed.

It was many weeks before we had any word from Bonnie and Clyde, long after we had come home and buried Buck. There were stories printed to the effect that Clyde would return for his brother's funeral; that he did return, disguised as an old woman, and wept beside the grave. In fact, by this time nothing was too wild, too fantastic and too unreal to be chalked up against Clyde Barrow. They made him a superman, gifted with super-human powers, beyond the reach of ordinary human beings. They made him a modern Frankenstein and fled in terror before the thing they had created.

Clyde and Bonnie showed up September 7, 1933. We had not seen them for four months, and what horrible and heartbreaking things had happened in those four months! Bonnie was still unable to walk without help. She was miserably thin and much older. Her leg was drawn up under her. Her body was covered with scars. Clyde also showed signs of what he had undergone. But they tried to make light of their condition. Clyde put a quilt on the ground and lifted Bonnie out of the car. I sat down beside her and held her thin hands and tried to keep the tears back. They talked of many things, but it was impossible to learn everything in one evening. It took many evenings.

They'd like some pillows, they said. They were living entirely in the car now, and they needed more pillows and some blankets, since the air was getting chilly. I suggested bringing Clyde's crutches out for Bonnie to use. We stayed late, and Clyde promised to meet us the next evening on the Eagle Ford Road. After we came home I took the pillows and blankets and crutches back to them.

They had not slept in a bed since July, or been inside a house. They had lived entirely in the car. At night they'd draw up in some side road and sleep, often being awakened by highway patrols and bawled out. On these occasions, Clyde would explain that they were touring and were so sleepy that they stopped for a nap. They were always believed, and sent on with a warning not to do it again, for fear somebody would run into them or hold them up.

On one occasion, Bonnie said only the fact that Clyde had become ill in the night had saved them from capture. He awakened her and after he felt better and dozed off to sleep, she heard a car coming. Something warned her that it was danger, so she stepped on the starter and swung off down the road driving. Looking in her rear vision mirror, she saw that the car was filled with policemen. She put on all speed, as they were definitely chasing her car. She called out to Clyde. Bonnie never learned to handle a car with the speed and daring that was Clyde's. Few people could.

"It's the law," she cried. "And they're gaining on us."

Clyde climbed over the seat, slipped under the wheel

while going fifty. He raised the speedometer to seventy, and shut off his lights. Trusting to luck, he roared along in the dark and turned up a gully. The officers, half a mile behind by now, passed by and lost him.

Bonnie said their best stunt was to drive into a town and run their car up on somebody's drive for the night.

This was their safest bet, for here they could sleep in security all night long. Cruising cops would deduce that the car belonged there and leave them alone. They used this means many times and were never caught but once. One night they had just stretched out nicely when they heard a wrathful feminine voice in the window above their heads: "John Jones, those lousy, whiskey- drinking, poker-playing friends of yours are parked out there in that drive again, but if you think you're going to sneak out of this house tonight — They never heard the rest of the dressing-down Mrs. Jones gave John, because they didn't wait.

One incident which amused Clyde greatly was the story of a Texas ranger, who with his wife, decided one night to run across the Red River bridge at Denison for a couple of bottles of beer. It was late and the ranger suggested that his wife go in her negligee. The man at the other end of the bridge sighted the ranger's guns lying in the back of the car and saw the woman in negligee. Before the ranger and his wife could get back across, the story was all over Denison that Bonnie and Clyde had just crossed Red River into Oklahoma.

Another night Clyde and Bonnie were at a sandwich shop getting their supper, when a car drove up containing four boys, who had obviously been imbibing a little too freely. One of the crew, a blustery sort of fellow, finally said: "If you all don't stop ragging me, I'll sic Bonnie and Clyde on you."

Hearing their names called like this, both Clyde and Bonnie leaned out, startled, and looked at the occupants of the other car. The speaker, seeing them, motioned largely with his hand and yelled: "That looks like Clyde and Bonnie there." Of course he was only joking, but Clyde thought he'd joke a little, too. He called out: "Come here, guy. I want to talk to you." The man climbed from the car and swaggered over. "What can I do for you?" he asked.

Clyde leaned close to him and spoke softly: "You can close your face," he said. "And keep it closed. I am Clyde Barrow and this is Bonnie Parker, and if you mention our names again, we'll drill you full of holes." The effect was startling. The man's mouth hung open, his eyes popped out, and he couldn't speak except to gurgle: "No, sir — no, sir." "You go back and get in the car and finish eating your order," Clyde told him. "Don't make a move and don't tell anything to anybody. If you do — !"

"But he was so scared he couldn't eat," Bonnie finished the story. "He just sat there with the sandwich in his hand, swallowing like he had a rock in his throat." I had moved into West Dallas now, and during the entire months of September and October, and up until Smoot Schmid tried to trap them on November 22, the kids came in to see us every single night except five. They'd either drive by the house or the filling station. Often they'd stop. Twice Clyde went in. If we didn't talk with them there they'd tell us where to meet them, and we'd drive out and be with them several hours. One evening Billie and I were sitting on the front porch chatting with a neighbor when Clyde and Bonnie came by. I didn't make any sign, but Billie got up and went into the house and out the back. My neighbor arose and said she'd better be getting on home. We walked down the alley and talked with Clyde and Bonnie for about thirty minutes. After they were killed my neighbor told me that she recognized them, but didn't want us to know she did, for fear something might happen and we would think she had turned them in.

It seems to me that it would have been such a simple matter to catch Clyde and Bonnie. All the law needed to do was to watch our houses, for they came in all the time, and we went out to see them. Of course, I didn't want them caught and I'm glad the officers were not smart enough to do it. For instance, there was Nell running a beauty parlor in the Sanger Hotel, headquarters for the Texas Rangers. Nearly every night for three months Nell drove to meet Clyde; almost every time he and Bonnie visited Dallas for two years, she was with them. Yet the rangers didn't even know that she was Clyde Barrow's sister till after his death, and I believe that she told them then. Clyde called Nell over long distance through the hotel switch board time after time, till she got frightened and made him use the shop number. If they had taken the trouble to find out that she was his sister, what would have been easier than tapping the telephone wire or checking up on Nell's long distance calls?

But, who am I to tell the police how they could have captured my daughter and Clyde? They got them in the end.

By now Billie had two children, Buddy, aged 4, and his sister, Jackie, who was 2. Jackie didn't remember much about Bonnie, as she was only a year old when Bonnie went away with Clyde. Buddy was very fond of her and talked of her often. When Jackie would start crying, Buddy used to say consolingly: "Don't cry, Jackie. Never mind. Bonnie's coming after awhile and sing the Craw Dad Song." We took Buddy to see Bonnie several times, and he was very wise for one so small. He said: "I shall tell my mother I have been with Bonnie, but nobody else." He never did, either.

On Christmas Clyde and Bonnie sent toys for the children. The Christmas of 1932, they bought a tricycle for Buster. Their funds were low, and driving along through a small town, they sighted a toy automobile on the lawn. Clyde got out and swiped it for Jackie. They hadn't gone a block before Bonnie asked: "How do you reckon that little kid will feel when he finds out his car is gone?"

"I guess he'll feel pretty bad," Clyde replied, and drove on a block. "I bet he'll cry," he said, and drove another block. Then: "Hell, we'll take it back!" They did.

On October 11, little Jackie took sick very suddenly. Two days later she died. I didn't go to meet Bonnie that night, but I was with them again on the following evening. Bonnie was heartbroken over the news. Sunday evening when I went to meet them I reported that Buddy was ill with the same strange malady — a stomach disorder. Monday night I reported that he was at Bradford Memorial Hospital, some better. I missed Tuesday night. When I met them Wednesday, Bonnie, her face white and tear-swept, said: "Don't tell me, mama. I know. Buddy's dead. I dreamed it last night. It was so real I knew it was true, and when Clyde started to buy toys to send him today, I wouldn't let him for I knew he wasn't alive any more."

Billie went all to pieces over this double tragedy. Our home was a bleak place indeed with the babies gone. Added to everything else, it seemed to us both that life wasn't worth the living any more. November 21 was the birthday of Clyde's mother. We took a birthday dinner and spent the day with Clyde and Bonnie up in Wise County, close to the Shannon farm. We were to meet them the next night at the place where Sheriff Smoot Schmid was to trap them. It was the first, last, and only time that we made the same meeting place twice. Just who knew and turned us in that night is still a mystery, but I'll never believe that the police: found out for themselves.

We drove to the spot just about dark. We could still see everywhere, but of course we couldn't see officers with machine guns hidden in a ditch. We were parked on the side road about seventy-five feet from the main highway. The officers were thirty feet away, concealed in the gully. In order to understand what I'm going to tell, the reader must try to get a mental vision of the lay of the land. We were parked facing away from the pike on the right side of the road. Before us this country road curved downward toward a little bridge, so that a car going down the road away from the highway would be out of range within a few seconds. It was still light enough for us to recognize Clyde and Bonnie when they drove along the pike. They started to turn in, but Clyde's sixth sense warned him.

"How do you feel about it, honey?" he asked. "It seems phony to me tonight."

They drove on down the pike a little way, but when we did not follow them, Clyde turned and came back, hesitated, and then cut into the lane. He had recognized us all right. He drove past us and started to turn around and come back and park beside us, as he said afterwards, but we didn't know this. We thought he wanted us to follow him, so we turned on our lights, making his car a direct target.

Something began popping. I said rather inanely: "Listen to the fire crackers." Then we saw the flame shooting out of the guns along the ditch. There was no word of "Halt!"—no warning given — nothing. They just began firing as Clyde was preparing to turn. Clyde stepped on the gas and shot away down the hill toward the bridge. We saw Bonnie break the back glass out of the coupe with her gun, although the officers said they shot it out. But she said when she did this, she cried out to Clyde: "I don't dare shoot. I'll kill my own mother if I do."

"If they haven't already done it," Clyde growled, for both of us women were screaming by now and they could hear us. "This whole road is probably lined with cops. Shoot at the ditches."

They bumped down the road, firing on each side as they went. At the bridge Clyde said: "You'd better pray, Bonnie. This is probably our last ride together." They both thought there would be more officers waiting for them there. The left tire had been shot away, and two bullets had passed through the car, one puncturing the spare, and the other entering Clyde's knee and going on through Bonnie's. They said they felt the impact but had no pain, and didn't know that they were wounded till later.

Bumping along on three tires, they covered the four miles to the next highway. The officers were unable to follow them, because they had parked their cars a mile away, but Clyde couldn't know that. Meanwhile, we had been forced to sit helplessly by and witness the whole thing. There was just one good thing about our having been there. We had seen it all, and we knew that Clyde's car disappeared over that hill after the first blast from the guns.

We went down to the court house later to look the car over after the officers had brought it in. The stories printed stated that a terrific gun battle had ensued between Clyde and Bonnie and Schmid and his men. The officers had ripped the car to bits with their guns, Clyde and Bonnie had fled, horribly wounded. Relatives were already making negotiations for funeral arrangements with local undertakers, since no person could have lived through the barrage put down on that car by officers that night.

We got a grim laugh out of that. Bonnie said the only reason they abandoned the car was because one tire and the spare were flat. They thought they were being pursued by other officers in cars, so they stopped two men on the highway in an old rattle trap Ford and told them to get out. When the owner refused, Clyde showed some expert marksmanship and put a hole through his hat. Clyde took only the guns from the coupe, since they had no time to waste. Bonnie was trying to start the car but couldn't find the switch. She asked the owner to show her where it was, but he seemed to feel that that was carrying good nature too far, and refused. "I guess you'll have to really shoot him," Bonnie said, and the man changed his mind again. He showed her where to find the switch. Some people stopped and asked Clyde if he needed any help, but he was doing nicely as it was, and advised them to keep driving and not look back. They took the hint. They abandoned the Ford in Oklahoma four days later.

It was very cold and the car was without windows. They had left their pillows and blankets in the other car, as well as their coats. They drove up a country lane, and came to a gate. Clyde got out to open it and fell.

Bonnie went to help him and fell also. They opened the gate, crawled back into the car and sat awhile. "We must be hit somewhere," Clyde said. "I can't walk."

"I can't either," Bonnie said. "But I don't hurt anywhere."

They stopped at a country filling station to get gas. Bonnie said that all the while the man was filling the tank, he stood looking down at the running board as if fascinated. She knew there were no bullet holes in the car to give them away, but at last she leaned over to see what was holding the man's attention. A rivulet of blood was trickling from under the door. After Clyde drove off, she said: "We're bleeding a lot — that's why we're so weak. We'd better get to a doctor."

They headed for Oklahoma. Here they received medical attention and stole another car with windows in it. They were back in Dallas on November 28, for Clyde had a score to settle. He was looking for Schmid's address. They drove to the Union Terminal and Clyde went in, presumably to use the 'phone. He took the telephone directory. Clyde was in a cold fury about the trap Schmid had laid for him.

"It wouldn't have mattered if he'd jumped us alone," he told us. "That's legitimate. We expect that. It's coming to us sooner or later. But to stage a gun battle with Bonnie's mother and my mother sitting there directly in range of the bullets — to start shooting when I wasn't ten feet away from their car — I'll get him for that. Why, he could have killed them both, and I'm out to get him."

That very night he and Bonnie drove out to Schmid's residence and waited till three in the morning, but either the sheriff was already safely in bed, or else he didn't come home that night. Clyde also waited for Bob Alcorn all one night without success. On another night he and Bonnie sat outside the county jail for two hours, checking on how many people came and went real early in the morning, and scouting the possibilities of snatching W. D. Jones from his cell, where he was dictating his memoirs to newspaper men.

Clyde was really blind with rage. He hated cops, it's true, but he'd kidnapped many officers when shooting would have been a simpler way out of it, if he'd really wanted to get rid of them permanently. This deliberate stalking of Schmid and Alcorn was the first time we'd ever known him to try to get a cop. Nell was the one who talked him out of it. Smoot Schmid and Bob Alcorn can thank Nell Barrow for the fact that they are alive and walking the streets of Dallas. Clyde had determined to kill them both.

Nell talked like a Dutch aunt to Clyde. There wasn't any use in arguing about the spot it would get Clyde in, because he didn't care. One murder more or less meant nothing to him. She put it up to him that others would be drawn into the trouble if he did this; that his family might become involved and held responsible. She pointed out that no possible good could result from his actions, and a lot of harm might come to innocent persons. They argued and argued. "But they might have killed mother!" Clyde yelled, getting red in the face. "They might have killed Bonnie's mother. Is that any way for men to fight — with women sitting by?" "They didn't kill anybody," Nell replied. "Let it skip, Clyde, let it skip."

The idea of getting W. D. out of the Dallas County jail was a big laugh to Nell. "You'd never get inside the place, Clyde," she told him.

"Oh, I don't know," Clyde said grimly. "I don't think it would be so hard. Harvey Bailey got out with a toy pistol. I think I could get in with a machine gun." Nell's contention was that it wasn't worth the effort, and that if W. D. were left alone long enough he would shoot up the place and walk out by himself. Clyde was out-talked, but his hatred for Schmid certainly never abated. Since Clyde had been ambushed by officers before and forced to fight his way out, yet had never sought to retaliate, it is reasonable to assume that he was earnest in his stand, and was furious at Schmid for violating what he termed his code.

It was along about this time that Clyde purchased the blonde woman's wig, which he used to wear when going through towns. Bonnie said she would paint his cheeks and rouge his lips and put one of her hats on him. "He made the cutest girl," she told us. "Our only trouble was that two blondes caused a commotion in traffic. When we'd stop for a red light, men would start giving us both the glad eye, so finally Clyde had to have the wig dyed black."

He used this means when forced to drive downtown, and for that reason often he and Bonnie went undetected through the principal streets of cities where their faces were well known and every traffic policeman was watching for them. They came and went in Dallas from the 28th of November till December 15th. Then we didn't see them till two days after Christmas, when they drove in with two gigantic baskets, beautifully packed, wrapped in cellophane, and tied with red ribbons and holly. They were filled with every kind of fruits, candies, and nuts imaginable. Bonnie said Clyde had them fixed especially for me and his mother at a fruit store in another state.

I said, "Honey, I couldn't enjoy my Christmas dinner, thinking of you and Clyde."

Bonnie laughed. "Why, mama, we had a lovely day," she told me. "We had two big turkey dinners in a cafe at Niles, Texas, and afterwards in Longview we bought a whole bunch of firecrackers — Roman candles, sparklers and some big cannon crackers. We went out in the country and spent the afternoon and evening shooting them off. We really had a grand time. You should not have worried."

They probably did all the things she said they did, but they didn't have a grand time. Bonnie and Clyde couldn't have a grand time anywhere, any more.

We saw them several times within the next few days, and then Clyde drove down to San Angelo. I don't know all the places he stuck up during this fall and winter, because he and Bonnie were headlined on big things and many of the smaller robberies were not credited to them by the police. I do know that Clyde held up a Piggly Wiggly store in Texas somewhere, because Bonnie said that they had one nickle when he went in to scout, and he bought gum with it. He came back and said there were too many people inside for him to try it alone. Bonnie said: "Well, how'll you go in anywhere else now? We've no more money to stall with." So Clyde said: "I'll go in with a gun." He did and took $100 out of the till.

Another time in November they robbed a refinery at Arp, Texas. When Clyde asked the men in the office for their money, one of them told him it was in a pipe in the wall. Clyde couldn't lift the pipe out, so he made them get it and give it to him. He put it in the car and drove out of town, took the money and threw the pipe away.

They spent days following a man who collected money each week from the A. and P. stores in the oil towns. They thought they had his itinerary all mapped out, and planned to hold him up after he'd made his rounds. When they stopped him, they discovered he had only been to two towns, and he told them the joke was on them, because he never went to the same towns twice in rotation.

We received an urgent message to meet them late one evening, and to bring some medicine for Bonnie, as she was sick. When we got out there, Bonnie was lying in the back seat of the car, looking like a ghost and crying. Clyde was holding her hand and looking mighty worried. "I don't know what's the matter with her," he said. "It seems to be something in her hip — not the one that was burned. It's the other leg."

"I was sitting on the running board down at San Angelo this morning, washing my face, when it hit me all of a sudden," Bonnie told Us. "All at once I started screaming."

"I'll say she started screaming," Clyde put in. "And she's been at it ever since. She couldn't sit up and she's screamed for hours. I brought her home, and I mean I've really brought her home if she doesn't get better." It sounded like rheumatism, so Nell prescribed a certain liniment and Clyde wrote it down. We gave her some aspirin and she got a little better. Clyde had just bought a new suit, and he put on the coat and got out in the headlights for us to look it over. It was about a fourth of an inch too long and he kicked up a great row about it. "I might as well bought an overcoat and been done with it," he stormed. "I'm going to take it right back and make them alter it."

Nell laughed at him. "What earthly difference does a quarter of an inch make?" she wanted to know. "Nobody ever sees it but Bonnie."

"Well, if you think I'm going to drive around with Bonnie, looking like Santa Claus, you're mistaken," he replied grimly. "And I'm going to dress my baby up tomorrow, too," he said.

Bonnie stuck her head up from the back seat long enough to remark: "A couple of pairs of pajamas will about fix your baby up fine, Mr. Barrow, the way she's feeling right now. Or make it one pair of pajamas and a dollar's worth of arsenic. Are you going to go buy that medicine, or not?"

Clyde drove off in a hurry and bought the medicine at Irving. Next day Bonnie was much better and Clyde was beaming. "Hi, Dr. Nell," he crowed. "That's the best damn medicine I ever saw. I'm going to buy a gallon and keep it in the car."

That was January 14. We spent two hours with them. On Monday, January 16, Clyde made the Eastham prison farm rescue and freed Raymond Hamilton, but he never breathed a word to us about it the whole time we were with them. He never did tell us anything till after it was executed. We then got the whole story.

Jimmie Mullens, a pal of Raymond Hamilton's, got out of Huntsville right after Christmas. Raymond had promised to pay him a thousand dollars if he'd help get him out of prison, so Mullens came to Dallas looking for a way to communicate with Clyde. He did not find this way through any of Clyde's or Bonnie's kin, but through another person who shall be nameless here. Raymond asked that Clyde leave guns under a certain small bridge near the Eastham farm. A trusty would bring them in and give them to Raymond. Saturday night after leaving us, Clyde and Bonnie picked up Mullens and drove to Huntsville, where they scouted over the lay of the land. While Clyde and Bonnie waited a mile and a quarter from the culvert, Mullens walked down and hid two forty-fives under the little bridge, according to arrangements.

Sunday was visiting day at the prison. Some visitor brought word to Raymond that the guns were there and that Clyde would be at a designated spot, over a mile away, on Monday morning, waiting for Hamilton and his friend, Bybee. Clyde would bring clothes for them to change into, but he would not drive down by the farm.

A heavy fog enveloped the country on Monday morning when the prisoners went to the fields. Raymond had the guns and had given one to Bybee. They made the break. There was no battle with machine guns, for Hamilton had no machine guns. Clyde and Bonnie did not put down a barrage to cover their getaway, for they were waiting a mile from the place.

Three other prisoners made a break with Hamilton and Bybee, and ran for the spot where Clyde and Bonnie were waiting. Clyde's only knowledge of the break was the sound of the guns in the heavy air, and the men crashing through the underbrush toward him and Bonnie.

As they neared the car, Hamilton, who was frightened of pursuit, yelled: "Let 'em have it, Clyde!" Clyde shot off about fifty rounds into the air in order to frighten pursuers, but there were none, as yet. Then Hamilton turned to the others and said: "Everybody go back except Bybee and me."

Clyde leaned out of the car and yelled: "No. Everybody hang on that can. I'll take you out." The five men were Hamilton, Bybee, A. B. French, Joe Palmer, and Henry Methvyn. Clyde's car was a turtle back, and he had bought clothes for two men only. Joe Palmer was sick, so he was given one suit to change into, and sat between Clyde and Bonnie in the front. The other four were stowed in the turtle back. They drove through Weldon without rousing any suspicion and without being stopped. At Hillsboro they bought gas, and the voluble attendant asked if they had heard the news about Clyde and Bonnie. He then regaled them with a highly dramatic and colorful story: Clyde and Bonnie had driven boldly up to the farm, cached machine guns in the ditches around the fields, held off dozens of armed guards with their own deadly fire, killing several and wounding many others, and took five desperate prisoners from the very arms of the guards. All roads were blocked with guns and police; every car was being stopped. There was no doubt but that the whole desperate bunch would be caught before night.

Clyde agreed with the man and drove off, heading for Houston. He had an idea that police in Dallas might just possibly be looking for him to come in. At Houston French left them. They drove on to Louisiana and four days later they arrived in Dallas to visit with us. Henry and Raymond were with them. Bybee had stolen a car and gone on his own. He was soon to be captured and returned to prison. I don't know where Joe Palmer was at this time. By this time thousands of officers all over Texas were watching for

Clyde, and roads were often barricaded and I know they were watched. Yet Clyde came through their lines like a will-o'-wisp and arrived in Dallas January 20. We drove out to meet Clyde and Bonnie that night. We had kodak, films, and pictures with us in the car. Out on the highway — we were heading out the Northwest — three policemen called to Nell to halt. We were all petrified with fear. We knew if they searched the car and found the pictures, they'd become suspicious, and when arrested and our names learned, we'd be in a spot. The officers said: "Start up." Nell started. "Now, stop!" he yelled. She stopped. "Back up!" he howled. Nell backed. "Go on," he said. "Just testing your brakes." We shook with fright for miles.

Raymond Hamilton was under obligations to Jimmie Mullens for $1,000. He and Clyde began planning to rob the Lancaster bank. In the meantime, Raymond wanted his girl, and she was sent for. We shall call her Alice, although that is not her name. Clyde didn't like her from the start. He said she was a stool pigeon. The boys waited a month before attempting the robbery at Lancaster. Then, with Bonnie and Alice waiting in a car on a side road, Henry, Clyde, and Raymond stuck up the bank for $2,400. Divided three ways, this gave $800 to each, and was not enough to clear off Raymond's obligation to Mullens. Henry always rode in front with Clyde and Bonnie. There was only Raymond and Alice on the back seat, and Clyde saw Raymond taking the money in his rear vision mirror. He said nothing about it to Raymond, but he told Bonnie, and they watched the pair constantly from then on.

Raymond was out after big dough. He was not content to rob filling stations and live from day to day. He wanted a lot of money and to live in style. When Clyde refused to rob any more banks for awhile, Raymond started in alone. He is credited, together with Clyde, of having stuck up the Mesquite Bank, March 3. Clyde said neither of them did it. Raymond did rob the Grand Prairie Bank and the bank at West. Clyde also had these two "hung on him," but told us he did not have anything to do with either.

Soon after this series of hold-ups, it is to be presumed that Raymond paid Mullens off. At any rate, the five of them headed north to get out of the hot atmosphere which surrounded them in Texas. Up north, somewhere in Indiana, the three boys ordered suits and overcoats, all tailored and matching. They also bought hats, shoes, and gloves to suit. The two girls purchased some dresses and coats. They attended shows, ate in good restaurants, and enjoyed themselves as well as the Clyde Barrows and Bonnie Parkers of this earth can enjoy themselves.

While they were gone, Clyde and Raymond broke up. There were many stories as to why they broke up, and the most romantic and colorful one is that it was over Bonnie Parker. It wasn't. They broke up over a girl, all right, but it was Raymond's girl, Alice. Clyde had never liked the girl, and he grew to like her less and less. After the split, Raymond wrote a letter to his lawyer in Dallas, for the press, in which he, in effect, requested all police officers to take note and put down in their books that Raymond Hamilton was a gentleman bandit, in no way to be connected with Clyde

Barrow, desperado, and that he was not operating with Clyde any more. Raymond seemed to have overlooked that the desperado, Clyde Barrow, had delivered him from the Eastham farm, and he was plenty good enough for that.

At any rate, this letter burned Clyde up, and he wrote one in reply. Only one, though two were received. Clyde had nothing to do with the letter written on a typewriter. Clyde had no typewriter, and the letter was not his. When Clyde replied to Raymond's open communication, he cited the rear vision mirror's view of Raymond lifting more than his share of the loot, and showed his dislike for Alice.

Up North Clyde would never leave Raymond and Alice alone for a minute. If they did not wish to attend shows with him and Henry and Bonnie, one of them stayed behind to keep them company. At last Raymond accused Clyde of not trusting him, and Clyde admitted that he didn't trust him or Alice.

The final break came when Clyde and Bonnie had a row. Bonnie was furious at Clyde and was "going home to mama" again. Alice sympathized with her. "I wouldn't put up with him," she stated. "I'd fix him, Bonnie."

"I'm going home," Bonnie sobbed. "I simply hate him."

"I'd fix him before I left," Alice told her.

"I'm going to," Bonnie insisted. "You wait and see." "I'd poison him," Alice went on.

"Poison him?" Bonnie cried, and whirled on her. "Poison Clyde?"

"Well, just dope him, then," Alice conceded. "Then while he's out, you can take his roll and beat it. Boy, think of the good time you could have on that money." "If I hadn't been so mad at Clyde, I believe I'd have slapped her," Bonnie told me. "But that finished me up with Alice. I told Clyde and he told Raymond that if Alice stuck around, it was all off. They split up right there, and we came back to Texas with Henry."

Bonnie told us this out on the Preston Road, where we'd gone to meet them in Nell's car. Bonnie needed a permanent and Clyde asked Nell to slip her into the shop late at night and give her one. "Good Lord," Nell cried in horror, "I wouldn't do it for a million dollars, Clyde. Why didn't she get one up North?"

"Sis, you ought to go to Indiana and open a beauty shop," Clyde replied. "You'd make a fortune. We drove three hours looking for one and never found it."

A car was coming down the main road; Nell got scared and tried to turn her car around, and ran off in the ditch. When the car had gone by, Clyde and Henry got out to pull her back on the road. Henry took barbed wire off a fence and tied Nell's car to the back of Clyde's. Clyde steered and Henry jerked her automobile to safety. When Clyde came back, wiping his hands from the grease, he grinned and said: "Sis, did you know you were practically walking? Why don't you buy yourself a decent car?"

"Beauty parlor operators don't get as much money as bandits," Nell replied, and Clyde yelled with laughter.

We weren't to see them again till a week after the Grapevine killing on April 1, 1934. The real reason back of that Grapevine murder is such a simple thing that the telling of it borders on the ridiculous. All the newspaper stories were wrong. The reports were that Raymond Hamilton, who had just robbed the bank at West, Texas, was to join Clyde and Bonnie on this side road. Clyde and Raymond hadn't been together for weeks, and there was no chance of their meeting this day. They were not parked there waiting for any gangsters. They had come to Dallas because Bonnie had a white rabbit which she wanted me to have for Easter, and they were waiting for both families to join them when the two officers drove up and were killed. They were not alone in the car. Joe Palmer and Henry Methvyn were with them when they first arrived, and Henry was there when the men were shot. Joe Palmer had gone to town to get word to us.

Bonnie bought the rabbit for me several days before Easter and she had had him in the car ever since. They named him Sonny Boy and Bonnie kept the car cluttered up with lettuce leaves and carrots for days. One afternoon, driving along, Clyde complained that Sonny Boy had acquired a peculiar odor, and had to have a bath if he was going to keep on riding with him. He found a little stream, took a cake of soap, and gave Sonny a very thorough scrubbing. Bonnie dried him with a towel and they started off again; but bathing didn't agree with Sonny Boy. He proceeded to pass out of the picture. Bonnie began bawling.

"He's dying," she sobbed. "You've killed my mama's rabbit with your old scrubbing."

"Oh, he'll come out of it," Clyde said, and kept on driving. Sonny Boy didn't come out of it. Bonnie's sobs shook the car.

"You would go and bathe him and he didn't smell — much," she snubbed.

"A little soap and water never hurt a rabbit yet," Clyde insisted, and kept on driving. Bonnie cried and Sonny Boy lay stiff and cold and wouldn't so much as wiggle a whisker. At last Clyde could stand it no longer. He turned down a side road, got out, gathered up a lot of dry wood and leaves and made a fire. He came back and got Sonny Boy and the weeping Bonnie. He thawed Sonny Boy out, and a time he had doing it, too. "I singed all my eyebrows off bringing that darned rabbit to," he told me.

After all this to-do, Clyde decided he wasn't going to allow a rabbit to run him crazy. They headed for Dallas to bring Sonny Boy to me. Joe Palmer and Henry were along. They stopped out near Grapevine and Joe got out and "thumbed" it into town to tell us where the kids would be. Nobody was at home at my house and nobody at Clyde's home except his father. Joe delivered the message. This was about one-thirty o'clock Sunday afternoon. They didn't get there till about one o'clock, and they didn't stay in the place where the officers were killed a great length of time. Clyde and Bonnie never told us a definite spot where they would meet us. They would say, "On the Eagle Ford Road," or "Mockingbird Lane," or "Preston Road." They usually just drove around and we'd meet them in the vicinity indicated. They drove around some this time, while waiting.

They had been in this lane but a short while when the shooting occurred. Newspapers stated that a man with guns and a girl in riding clothes had been parked in the lane all day. They had done target practice, eaten their lunch on the fender and made open love to each other. When the two officers arrived, both had opened up with machine guns, killing them. The girl then ran to where one dying officer lay and kicked him over, pumping lead into his helpless body. The two drove away laughing.

This is how the kids related it: Bonnie was letting Sonny Boy eat grass along the road. Clyde, becoming sleepy, took a nap in the back of the car. Henry walked up and down. They had no lunch, neither did they do target practice. "That would have been a smart trick," Clyde remarked, when he read the account in the papers. "Wanted for a dozen things by every cop in Texas and then I'd get out on a country road and shoot off guns. Damn smart! " Clyde and Bonnie rarely, if ever, made love before people. I never saw Clyde kiss Bonnie but three times in my life. Besides, they had been together for two years now, and it wasn't likely they'd be making exhibitions of their devotion for Henry Methvyn or any other person. Neither Clyde nor Bonnie were out of the car when the two officers, E. B. Wheeler and H. D. Murphy, turned into the lane that afternoon.

Bonnie got back into the front seat with Sonny Boy by this time, and was brushing his fur. She heard the noise and leaned and shook Clyde. "It's the law," she whispered. Clyde jumped up and looked out quickly. Henry had moved back by the side of the car where the guns were lying. The officers had ridden in and were leisurely racking their motorcycles, apparently with no thought of danger. They had not drawn their guns and were evidently not expecting any trouble.

"Let's take 'em," Clyde said.

Henry Methvyn had been with Clyde only a short time and had never been in a situation where Clyde had kipnapped officers before. To him, "Let's take 'em," meant only one thing. Of course, he was badly frightened. He was an escaped convict and wanted for a number of things. Also, he and Bonnie had been drinking. He seized the guns, whirled and fired a steady volley. Both men crumpled to the ground without a sound, their guns still in their holsters. Bonnie was petrified with fear and Clyde was white with rage. He was cursing furiously as he slid over the seat and under the wheel.

"Get in here, you damn fool!" he cried. "Now you've done it."

"But it was them or us," Henry protested, looking at Clyde in amazement.

"Like hell!" Clyde exploded. "They didn't know who we were. Tell me! There's not a pair of cops in the whole country with guts enough to come after Clyde Barrow alone. They'd never have turned in that lane if they'd known I was down here."

This may sound like bragging on Clyde's part, but bragging or not, he said it. When officers came to get Clyde, as newspapers told it, they came in droves with armored cars, machine guns, and shields. If Wheeler and Murphy had known that Clyde was up that country lane, they'd probably be alive today.

Clyde ran for it. It was all they could do. Bonnie told me that Clyde swore at Henry for two days because of the blunder he had made. Not that Clyde was against killing policemen, but simply that he saw no sense in doing it unless it had to be done.

We got in from White Rock about 3:30 that afternoon. Clyde's father gave us the message and we drove right on out to Grapevine. We knew nothing of the shooting and considered it rather peculiar that the highway was lined with officers with machine guns. We drove up and down for several hours, still not knowing what had happened. We did not go near the lane where the killing occurred because we did not know they had been there. When it began to get dark we came back home. As soon as we got home we were informed of the tragedy. Clyde's father said someone had heard it over the radio and had telephoned him. We didn't believe that Clyde and Bonnie had done it at all. It didn't sound a bit like them. Bonnie had never worn men's clothes; she didn't like them, and since the injury to her leg, she was unable to wear tight-fitting clothes. We just didn't believe that she'd so wantonly kill a person. The whole thing sounded phony, so we decided that someone else had done this awful deed and the kids had beat it because they dared not stay.

On Saturday, April 6, less than a week from the Easter killing, Clyde, Bonnie, and Henry were again in the papers. This time they had killed Constable Cal Campbell at Commerce, Oklahoma, and had kidnapped the police chief, Percy Boyd. We believed that story because it sounded just like them. But we didn't learn details till a week later when Clyde and Bonnie came back to Texas. They came on April 17.

On this Saturday, the two boys were sleeping in the car by the roadside outside of Commerce. Bonnie was keeping watch in the front seat, holding the white rabbit. A farmer with a cow in a truck drove along. Bonnie didn't waken Clyde because she said she felt sure the farmer didn't recognize them and wouldn't report them. The farmer didn't know who they were, but he reported them just the same. He hunted up Constable Campbell and informed him that two drunks were out on the highway asleep and there was a girl with them. Cal Campbell found the chief of police Percy Boyd, having a shave in a barber shop. They took their time getting under way. Drunks were often troublesome, but they weren't exciting.

Bonnie saw them coming and called to Clyde. He slid over the seat and under the wheel, still in his sock feet. He meant to run for it. In his haste to turn around, he backed off into the ditch and stuck. The officers alighted with drawn guns and came forward. Clyde and Henry started firing. Cal Campbell fell, and Boyd raised his hands over his head in token of surrender. Both men were rather old and certainly hadn't come looking for trouble. Clyde made Boyd get into the car. Then, while Bonnie held a gun on him, the two boys tried to get the car out of the ditch. Another car came along and stopped to ask if they could help. Clyde used his gun to hasten matters. The men hurriedly put the car back on the pavement. Clyde raced away with

Boyd in the back seat beside Henry.

After half an hour of terrific driving, Boyd inquired timidly of Henry: "I don't like to get personal, but isn't that Clyde Barrow? " Henry said it was.

Bonnie and Boyd struck up quite an acquaintanceship. He told her about his family and she told him about hers. She also asked him, if anything happened to her while he was in the car, would he see that her mama got the white rabbit? Boyd promised.

"We liked him," Bonnie said. "When we let him out, we gave him a new shirt and tie and expense money back home. He asked me: 'Bonnie, what shall I tell the world when I go back?' And I said, 'Tell them I don't smoke cigars!' He did it, too. It was in all the Oklahoma newspapers." This pleased Bonnie greatly.

They drove to Topeka that day, and circled back to Dallas about the middle of April. At Wichita Falls, Henry Methvyn got out and took the train. He was coming down to tell us where to meet Clyde and Bonnie this time. On the train from Wichita Falls Henry rode with Texas Rangers. They were friendly and soon Henry joined in the conversation. He told us that all their talk was of the Grapevine killing and Bonnie and Clyde. He said his hair stood on end when they speculated as to where Henry Methvyn and the two kids could be.

When he arrived in Dallas it was early morning. Henry went down to the Sanger Hotel and walked up and down in front of the shop, but Nell wasn't down yet. He debated calling her apartment and decided against it.

Failing to find Nell, Henry walked on out to find me and Clyde's mother. One of the first things he said to me was: "Mrs. Parker, I killed those two officers at Grapevine! " Later that day at Mount Pleasant, Bonnie told me this, too, but Henry told me first. My white rabbit was delivered to me that trip. I still have him. "Keep him away from the cops," Bonnie said, when she gave him to me. "He's been in two gun battles and he'll land at Huntsville if the law finds it out."

Clyde was still angry with Henry about the Grapevine murder. Not from the standpoint of murder, but from the standpoint of a senseless murder. "He didn't have to kill them," he insisted* "They didn't suspect a thing — just racked their motorcycles and never even drew a gun. We could have taken 'em for a ride. Such a damn fool stunt." Bonnie finally made him hush. What was done was done, she said, so let it go.

That day we begged Clyde and Bonnie to leave the country. It seemed beyond human endurance that we could go on living through the horrors we were enduring; we didn't see how they could, either. The endless strain was telling on them and it was certainly killing us. The end was so inevitable. They hadn't a chance — not a chance in the world. Death was waiting for them. It was at their very heels. We begged them to run for the border; try to get across and start all over again. "You know you're going to get it and get it soon," we said. "Aren't you afraid?"

"Sure, we're afraid," Clyde replied. "We never know what the next hour will bring. You may think this is funny — but we never go through a town or past a place where there may be a trap, that we don't pray we'll make it."

I didn't think that was funny. Every human being, when desperate, turns to God, no matter what sort of lives they may have led. Bonnie and Clyde had their backs to the wall; they could depend on nothing now except their own swiftness, courage and cunning. They were worn out with the fight. They were outlawed to the world and to society. Every hand was against them, and justly so. There was no earthly help toward which they might turn, so they prayed. It wasn't funny to me. It was tragic.

We tried all of our arguments that day; we used every persuasion we could muster to get them to leave Texas forever, but they refused. "Seeing you folks is all the pleasure Bonnie and I have left in life now," Clyde said. "Besides each other, it's all we've got to live for. Whenever we get so we can't visit our people, we might as well die and be done with it. We're staying close to home and we're coming in as long as we're alive."

They had a plan, too, whereby we could be with them all summer. They said they wanted to buy a house on Henry Methvyn's father's land down in Louisiana, and fix it up so that we could come down and visit with them. Then at nights they'd slip in and be with us. We listened to their enthusiastic planning with an apathetic numbness. It would be the same old thing again: secret meetings, signals, constant fear like a black shadow over everything; and then some night out of the stillness a terrific barrage of machine gun fire from some ditch or gully. But we let them plan.

When we were convinced that we could not change them, we turned our talk to lighter things and tried to enjoy the afternoon. Clyde had a bunch of clippings he'd saved from Dallas newspapers, and he got a big kick out of them. There were several cartoons and some squibs from columnists. One cartoon showed the sheriff asleep, snoring, while Clyde and Bonnie poked their heads out from under his bed. Another was of Pretty Boy Floyd surrounded by newspapers featuring Clyde and Bonnie. Pretty Boy was jumping up and down and yelling: "I haven't had any publicity in weeks." The squibs were all jibes at the Dallas authorities for their failure to apprehend Clyde and Bonnie. One read: "Clyde and Bonnie give Smoot Schmid twenty-four hours to get out of town." Another said: "Clyde and Bonnie let Smoot Schmid get away again."

Clyde thought all these ridiculous pictures and stories were very funny, but they were merging into a tide of sentiment which was to sweep over the two of them on a May morning in Louisiana and leave death behind. Officers had been kidded about Clyde and Bonnie long enough; too long, to suit their sense of humor. They meant to get them and they did.

We saw them for the last time on Sunday evening, May 6. They drove by the filling station in West Dallas and told us where to meet them. They had chosen a spot four miles east of Dallas on a country road. We went out and were with them about two hours, I guess. I sat on the ground under the stars and talked to Bonnie for a long time that night. I remember that as she talked, she was showing me some new snapshots she and Clyde had taken.

"Mama," she began, with that peculiar calm which she and Clyde were always in when speaking of death, "when they kill us, don't let them take me to an undertaking parlor, will you? Bring me home."

I reached out and seized her wrist and jerked her toward me. "Don't, Bonnie, for God's sake!" I cried. I wanted to scream.

There she sat, so young, so lovely — only twenty-three — with the May moonlight sifting through her yellow hair and making shadows on her cheeks — there she sat and talked to me of death as calmly as if she were discussing going to the grocery store. Bonnie looked up at me and smiled. It was a funny smile — as if she were a million years older than I was; as if she knew things that I'd never learn if I lived for centuries; as if this flutter I was making about the talk of death was rather childish and so to be excused.

"Now, mama, don't get upset," she said to me. "Why shouldn't we talk it over? It's coming — you know it — I know it — all of Texas knows it. So don't let them keep me at the undertakers. Bring me home when I die — it's been so long since I was home. I want to lie in the front room with you and Billie and Buster sitting beside me. A long, cool, peaceful night together before I leave you. That will be nice — and restful." She turned one of the pictures toward me. "I like this one," she went on calmly. It was a picture of Clyde holding her up in his arms. They were both laughing. Bonnie's red lacquered fingers caressed the surface of the picture slowly. "And another thing, mama," she went on, "when they kill us, don't ever say anything — ugly — about Clyde. Please promise me that, too."

I promised her, and I kept my promise where Clyde was concerned, but the people of Dallas would not let me keep the other one. Bonnie never came home when she died, because I could not bring her through the crowds, and she could have had no peaceful night if I had brought her. My little street was black with people that night and it took a cordon of police for me to get through.

On this last meeting, I recall that Billie was very cross because I had refused to let her do something she'd set her heart on doing, and she told Bonnie about it. Bonnie looked at her baby sister. "I just wouldn't pay any attention to mama if I were you, Billie," she said.

Billie fairly gasped at this treason and looked from Bonnie to me and then back again. "You wouldn't?" she echoed.

Bonnie shook her head. "No, I'd just go right ahead and do as I pleased," she told Billie. "I wouldn't mind mama at all."

"Why, Bonnie! " Billie cried. "I'm ashamed of you." "Just take a look at me," Bonnie went on. "I'm a shining example of what happens when a girl doesn't mind her mother. You just go right ahead, Billie, and see where you land." She laughed when she said it. It wasn't a bitter laugh but it was a little brittle, like falling glass.

Bonnie gave me the poem that night, "The Story of Bonnie and Clyde." I shall present it here because it gives a little of the inside angle of the case. Clyde and Bonnie bade us all good-bye — their last good¬bye — and drove away. They would be back in two weeks, they promised. But in two weeks they were dead.

The Story of Bonnie and Clyde

You've read the story of Jesse James —
Of how he lived and died;
   If you're still in need
   Of something to read
Here's the story of Bonnie and Clyde.

Now Bonnie and Clyde are the Barrow gang.
I'm sure you all have read
   How they rob and steal
   And those who squeal
Are usually found dying or dead.

There's lots of untruths to these write-ups;
They're not so ruthless as that;
   Their nature is raw;
   They hate all the law —
The stool pigeons, spotters, and rats.

They call them cold-blooded killers;
They say they are heartless and mean;
   But I say this with pride,
   That I once knew Clyde
When he was honest and upright and clean.

But the laws fooled around,
Kept taking him down
And locking him up in a cell,
  Till he said to me,
  "I'll never be free,
So I'll meet a few of them in hell."

The road was so dimly lighted;
There were no highway signs to guide;
  But they made up their minds
  If all roads were blind,
They wouldn't give up till they died.

The road gets dimmer and dimmer;
Sometimes you can hardly see;
  But it's fight, man to man,
  And do all you can,
For they know they can never be free.

From heart-break some people have suffered;
From weariness some people have died;
  But take it all in all,
  Our troubles are small
Till we get like Bonnie and Clyde.

If a policeman is killed in Dallas,
And they have no clew or guide;
  If they can't find a fiend,
  They just wipe their slate clean
And hang it on Bonnie and Clyde.

There's two crimes committed in America
Not accredited to the Barrow mob;
  They had no hand
  In the kidnap demand,
Nor the Kansas City Depot job.
A newsboy once said to his buddy:
"I wish old Clyde would get jumped;
  In these awful hard times
  We'd make a few dimes
If five or six cops would get bumped."

The police haven't got the report yet,
But Clyde called me up today;
  He said, "Don't start any fight —
  We aren't working nights —
We're joining the NRA."

From Irving to West Dallas viaduct
Is known as the Great Divide,
  Where the women are kin,
  And the men are men,
And they won't "stool" on Bonnie and Clyde.

If they try to act like citizens
And rent them a nice little flat,
  About the third night
  They're invited to fight
By a sub-gun's rat-tat-tat.

They don't think they're too smart or desperate,
They know that the law always wins;
  They've been shot at before,
  But they do not ignore
That death is the wages of sin.

Some day they'll go down together;
They'll bury them side by side;
  To few it'll be grief —
  To the law a relief —
But it's death for Bonnie and Clyde.

On Saturday, May 19, Billie, who was working in a cafe at Gladewater, was arrested by officers as the girl who had done the killing at Grapevine on Easter Sunday. Despite the testimony of my sister, my daughter- in-law, myself, and Clyde's mother that Billie had been home all day Easter Sunday, Billie was taken to Ft. Worth and put in a cell.

I was frantic about this new development. You can imagine how we felt with Bonnie an outlaw and the fingers of justice reaching out to snare my other daughter. Billie was still in jail when the news came that Clyde and Bonnie had been killed eight miles from Gibsland in Bienville Parish, Louisiana, at 9:15 the morning of May 23. I received the news about 9:30.

I remember that I was sewing. All the family were at home except Billie. This new tragedy had drawn us together. In spite of the fact that I had told myself over and over again that I was ready to meet their death when it came, I found that I was not. A newspaper reporter called me and asked me if I were alone. I replied in the negative. He then asked to talk with my sister or my son. Reporters were always calling up to get stories and statements, and I told him he could ask me whatever he wanted to know. The man insisted on speaking to some other member of the family, and after a rather warm argument, during which time I was very stubborn and lost my temper, he blurted out the news of the killing. I dropped the receiver and began crying. As soon as Buster heard it, he said it wasn't true — that we had received dozens of such messages and they had never been true. But something told me that this time it was the truth.

The undertaker arrived to get some one to go with him to Arcadia. I wanted to go but Buster wouldn't let me. He went instead. Clyde's father accompanied another undertaker to bring back Clyde's body. They left around noon. Buster got lost and didn't arrive at Arcadia till ten that night.

Bonnie and Clyde had been dead thirteen hours, yet the dried blood had never been washed from their bodies, and they still lay, unclothed, in the undertaker's parlor, a back room in a furniture store. The morbidly curious were filing past in a constant stream. They had broken out the plate glass windows of the store, and ruined the stock of furniture. The undertaker said he had not been able to embalm the bodies properly because of the crowds. He was able to keep them back by squirting embalming fluid on them, which was rather an expensive process. Officers of the law offered no aid in controlling the mobs.

Of course, it was an open secret that some one whom Clyde and Bonnie had trusted, had betrayed them. The newspapers were full of it; the town of Arcadia was crawling with rumors to that effect. Officers and Rangers spoke guardedly and gave non-committal answers to reporters. It was not hard to piece the facts together and get the answer.

When we went down after the funeral, some of the country people took us to the house where Clyde and Bonnie were supposed to have lived. Nothing could make me believe that they had lived there. Clyde and Bonnie were so particular about being clean, and this was a filthy hole, with old feed sacks on the floor, and trash and dirt everywhere. There was no glass in the windows and the doors wouldn't close properly. Besides, the house was situated in a spot that was a perfect trap. A single narrow road led down through the pines to it. Clyde Barrow was too clever to have holed himself up in this place, where he could be taken easily and have no chance for flight. Clyde's head worked in times of danger and in times of peace. He always saw to it that there was a good exit. There was no exit here. Just where they did stay is something we don't know, but I'm convinced it was not in this house.

On this morning of May 23, Clyde and Bonnie had driven into town and Bonnie bought a magazine. Probably Clyde purchased supplies. About eight miles out of Gibsland on a little hill, Clyde and Bonnie came upon Henry Methvyn's father. He had stopped his truck and taken the wheel off. He had a puncture, so he said. Clyde parked his car beside the truck and got out to see if he could help. This put the Methvyn truck between Clyde's car and the officers, hidden 100 yards away in the underbrush. Bonnie was sitting in the front seat reading her magazine. For once Clyde's sixth sense wasn't working. He had released Henry Methvyn from Eastham prison farm; Henry had been with him on several robberies and in two gun battles where officers were killed, and therefore Clyde sensed no danger.

Another truck loaded with logs came up the hill and blew the horn for Clyde to move over. Clyde got back in his car and pulled up in front of Mr. Methvyn's truck, and started to back closer. This was what the officers were waiting for. Without a word of warning they all came down with a barrage of machine gun fire. Clyde's last act was to shift the gears into low for a get-away and to reach for his gun.

The first blast from the officers' guns struck Clyde full in the head and the left side. He slumped forward over the wheel. It also ripped Bonnie's body to ribbons and she too fell forward just as the car left the road, careened into a sandbank, and stopped. The officers ran out into the road, still firing. They let loose another blast into the rear and side of the car, in order to make doubly sure. Then they approached the toppled car warily, guns ready to fire again.

Although they had already poured enough lead into both bodies to have killed fifty men, they still doubted that the couple was dead. They were expecting momentarily to hear the rat-tat-tat of returning fire, and to behold Clyde Barrow, the charmed and unkillable, behind the car with a machine gun, ready to fight it out again. But this time there really was no danger.

They reached the car, jerked the door open, and looked inside. A Browning automatic was between Clyde's knees, but his hand had been shot away from his grasp on the weapon. Bonnie, an automatic pistol in her lap, was crumpled over her magazine. Over fifty bullet holes were in each body. They were both quite dead. The long chase was over. The law had won. Bonnie and Clyde would never stand the world off again, two against death, for death had overtaken them at last.

Epilogues

Although their death is really the end of the story, perhaps the reader would like to know the details of the burial, so we add this final word as told by Mrs. Parker:

The horrible things which occurred both in Arcadia and Dallas, following the death of Bonnie and Clyde, were the sort of revolting episodes which shake one's faith in civilized humanity. We didn't expect people to have respect for Bonnie Parker and Clyde Barrow. They were due no respect. But the state of death deserves respect in any land, and this was denied them.

Dr. Wade, the coroner at Arcadia, related afterwards that when he arrived at the scene of the killing two hours after it occurred, officers were still milling around. A crowd of several hundred had gathered about the death car, and Bonnie's dress, which was shot to ribbons, was almost cut from her back by curiosity seekers who were gathering souvenirs. Clyde's blood stained shirt and undershirt were in the same condition. We still have these garments, bearing mute testimony to the truth of this statement. Bonnie's hair had been clipped away, also, and some one was trying to get her diamond rings off her fingers. One man was reported to have been rifling Clyde's pockets when the coroner and undertaker arrived. They stopped him. Other people had ripped open the trunk on the back of the car and scattered its contents. Some enterprising onlooker was attempting to remove a hub cap from a wheel. Every piece of broken glass was eagerly picked up. The spot where the officers had lain in wait was trampled level by those who hunted for empty shells to take away. The crowds even cut down the trees and dug bullets from them. Bonnie and Clyde always divided what money they had evenly, but someone evidently rifled Bonnie's purse because, while Clyde had $500 in his pockets, only a few dollars was found in Bonnie's possession. I was told by a man who was there that he stopped some unknown person in an attempt to cut Clyde's ear off. This person wanted to preserve it in alcohol, he said.

The bodies were not brought to Arcadia till noon, and then the undertaker was held up two hours for the inquest. The undertaker told me that he put Clyde's wrist watch and diamond stick pin in a box when he took them off, but when he went to look for them to give to Clyde's people, the stick pin was gone; it had been taken by some one else. Nothing was done about it. We never received their personal belongings, except what they had on when killed, and a few clothes wrapped in a newspaper. They had laundry and clothes in a Shreveport cleaning plant with a bill of $14 against them. We never received these things, either.

When the bodies arrived in Dallas on the morning of May 24, people behaved in about the same manner as they did in Arcadia, but the Dallas police made an effort to control them. Twenty thousand people jammed the street in front of the funeral home where Bonnie lay, and almost as many came to view Clyde. It was a Roman holiday. Hot dog stands were set up; soda pop vendors arrived to serve those who waited to view all that was left of the South's most noted desperadoes.

The final grim and sardonic touch was the great loads of flowers that arrived. It was impossible to hold the crowds back and they were wrecking both the place where Bonnie lay and the establishment where Clyde had been taken. Some newsboys contributed money for wreaths for Clyde and Bonnie. A small bouquet of lilies arrived with a note asking that they be placed in Bonnie's hands that night. The sender said another bouquet would be sent the following day when these flowers had wilted, and asked that the wilted bunch be saved and given to me. This was done. I don't know who the person was.

I had carried small life insurance policies on all of my children for many years. For this reason I was able to bury Bonnie as I wished. She had the loveliest blue silk negligee that money could buy. It matched her blue eyes. Her hair was marcelled and her nails polished. Her casket was of silver, and she was buried holding the lilies from the unknown sender.

We did not have the funeral till Saturday, following her death on Wednesday. We delayed because we were bending every effort to have Billie released long enough to be present. This was not accomplished till Saturday morning. The following Thursday, ballistic tests proved Billie innocent of the charge of murder and she was formally freed.

We planned to bring Bonnie home on Friday night. They tried to talk me out of it, but I was determined. "It was her last request," I said. "She wanted to come home and she's coming home."

They asked me then to look out of the door at the crowds who were waiting at my home. I realized the hopelessness of the attempt and gave it up. A car with police escort was sent to bring me to the funeral home. We fought our way in. We had lived through so many things far worse than death during the past two years that none of this penetrated to our minds. We were finally past being hurt by anything.

I didn't look at Bonnie till she was in her casket, and even then it was a terrible shock because of what the bullets had done to her little red mouth. At first she was a stranger to me. But the longer I looked, the more her features became normal. It was a miracle which probably came from my own imagination to save my sanity. Slowly, beneath my gaze her face changed till she was once more Bonnie as I had known her — the same little girl who used to pat my slippers lovingly as she put them away; the same sweet child who had sung the Craw Dad Song to Billie's little boy.

I looked down at her and I thought: "Your troubles are over now, baby. You died with the man you loved. Thank God it's over at last. Thank God you'll never run and hide and steal and kill and suffer in pain, and cry for your mother again. Thank God — thank God —" Then merciful blackness came up to blot my vision and I remembered nothing for a long time.

We buried Clyde on Friday afternoon and Bonnie on Saturday — not together, as they had wished. Each family wanted the privilege of placing the body in its own private burial plot. Bonnie was laid to rest beside Billie's babies; Clyde sleeps with his brother, Buck. Both funerals were nightmares. Nell was unable to get within forty feet of Clyde's grave. While the curious fought their way toward the grave side, as a last fantastic touch, aviators swooped low and dropped flowers on the bier. All this hysteria, for and against, was enough to make one lose one's reason and go mad laughing. But none of us cared. We were past caring. The long trail had ended. Bonnie and Clyde had sinned and suffered and paid the price. They had broken the laws of God and man, and Death had come out to meet them on a morning in May —D eath for Bonnie and Clyde.

[THE END]

Index

V

Vallie, Virginia 65
Victoria, Texas 137
Vidor, Florence 65
Villa, Pancho 14

W

Waco, Texas 43, 81- 83, 85, 86, 92-
    93, 96
Wayne, John 10
Weldon, Texas 96
Wellington, Texas 147, 175-179,
    181-182, 189
Western Union 25
West, Texas 230, 233
Wharton, Texas 137, 170
Wheeler, E. B. 235
White Rock 237
Wichita Falls, Texas 37-38, 119, 121,
    126, 239
Wilson, Weber 185
Winslow, Arkansas 186
Wise County, Texas 217
Wooster, Massachusetts 104, 117

Y

Younger, Cole 14, 21

CPSIA information can be obtained
at www.ICGtesting.com
Printed in the USA
LVHW102136170922
728642LV00003B/50